The Vision of A Middle Class Man

ACKNOWLEDGEMENT

This book is dedicated to the Almighty and my parents.

About the Book

This book is not only a vivid guide to making the most out of your passion of travelling even when you belong to a humble background, but also a heartfelt memoir of the life of a middle-class man. It is the narration of the experiences of the author as he anchors his responsibilities as the head of the family while also being the person who fulfils his own desire and follows his passion. The book cruises through decades of achievements, big and small; through rivers of smiles and tears alike; as the author travels through the world, taking the readers along with him on this beautiful journey. The book is nothing but the journey of the dream of a child that was most graciously brought to fruition during his adulthood. All the events mentioned in the book are real instances from the author's life presented to the reader with utmost sincerity and frankness.

About the Author

Prabodh Ranjan Padhee is a passionate traveller and writer who hails from the small steel town of Rourkela. He completed graduation in Mechanical Engineering from Regional Engineering College, Rourkela (Presently National Institute of Technology, Rourkela) in the year 1980. He joined the public sector company, Steel Authority of India Limited (SAIL) as a Management Trainee that very year and superannuated in 2018 as the Chief General Manager (Erstwhile General Manager) of Rourkela Steel Plant, SAIL. He went on to co-author a book titled *"Process Modelling for Steel Industry"*, which has become an acclaimed book for steel industry and academic perspective. He has also published various articles in reputed international journals such as Wiley and Springer Nature. He has served as the Guest Faculty of several reputed institutions all over India and is a regular panellist in various seminars and webinars. He has also presented papers in International Conference, which has been published by Springer Nature. This book is his debut *"Non-fiction"* book, where he has attempted to amalgamate his greatest passion, which is **travelling and writing**, in the honest possible manner.

About the Editor

Sanskruti Pujari is a student, currently pursuing her Master's degree in English Literature. She indulges in reading and collecting books, writing poetry, and learning languages. She is focused on building a career in academics and works as a content writer in her leisure time.

<u>PREFACE:</u>

A child was born in 1958 in a middle-class family in a small town in the western part of Odisha, Rourkela. His father came to Rourkela in 1955 from, again a small-town, Sambalpur, after his graduation, to start his career in the Finance Department of Rourkela Steel Plant. During the 2nd Five-year plan of the Government of India, the construction of the first integrated steel plant had started, which is the Rourkela Steel Plant. That child born in 1958, was none other than myself & just after my birth, my father was selected for a 2 years' residential course on Finance Management at Calcutta (Present Kolkata), organised by his employer Rourkela Steel Plant, Hindustan Steel Limited. After completion of Finance Management, my father, rose to a reasonably higher position in the organisation. I am the youngest child of my parents, among the three and both my brothers are elder to me. Right from my childhood, I had a vision of visiting & seeing the whole world. Keeping that in mind, how I achieved and accomplished this vision of mine, despite limited resources, financial and social constraints, has been described in this book.

My passion for travelling has led me to visit several places ranging from hills to sea beaches. My primary focus as a passionate traveller was to travel abroad and see different places all over the world and learn about their culture. In this book, I have focused primarily on my foreign travel. I have also included few experiences of my travel within the country which might equally fascinate the reader. My family would often accompany me during my travels which made my experiences more memorable.

I have described some of my most fascinating experience with in the India, which are as follows: In the North, it was my flight from Delhi to Kullu in the 'Jagson Airlines' in May 2003. It was a 22-seater unpressurised aircraft. Kullu airport is a table top, a very small runway, with the mountains on one side and the river Beas on the other side. In addition to that, Manali and Rohtang Pass were fascinating because of the white snow and the sight of children skiing on it. Another nice place was Mussoorie and then the Clubhouse experience in "Naini lake", Nainital in 2014 was unforgettable. The Clubhouse is right in the middle of the lake and having a glass of beer with awesome food while enjoying the beauty of the lake and the surrounding from the window, was something different. In the same year, my visit to the city of Rishikesh, bathing in the clear and chilling water of River Ganges, was something different. Again, during this July'2021, staying at a resort about 40 km beyond Rishikesh named "Neemrana Glass House" by the side of Ganges, was out of the world. The experience of Udaipur and Mount Abu in Rajasthan, in 2018, was also just great. There, I found a combination of Indian history and heritage along with the beauty of nature which I enjoyed. I started my tour of Southern India with a hill station named 'Kodaikanal', in 1986. I remember it as a quiet and serene place. That was followed by my visit to Pondicherry in 1999. In 2002, I had the pleasure of visiting 'The jewellery of the Nizam' at the Salarganj museum and the 'Dancing fountain' in Lumbini Park, Hyderabad. I also visited the 'Brindavan Gardens' at Mysore in the same year. To the east, in 1984, I had visited Darjeeling. I visited places like Bodh Gaya, Nalanda, Rajgir, and PawaPuri in the year 1993, with my parents. I had the good fortune of visiting the 'Dakshineswar Kali' in 2010. My home state, Odisha, gave the wildlife lover within me ample reasons to be happy about. I explored dolphins, several migratory birds, and wildlife in places such as 'Satapada' in the Chilika Lake, again a wetland named 'Mangalajodi' in the Northern edge of the Chilika, and the Debrigarh Sanctuary in the dense forests near Sambalpur respectively. The highlight of my travels in Western India was a place called 'Matheran', in 2009, a place near Mumbai that I found to be unique. The place was a polythene-free zone and no vehicular movement was allowed. One could see the clouds, rather touch the clouds, which was exhilarating. My Bombay (now Mumbai) and Goa trips in 1984 have been narrated in detail later in this book.

During the Corona Pandemic outbreak in India and national lockdown, it became mandatory to stay at home for months together. I tried to make the most of this time by writing this book which I believe will help others to dream big. Despite being a middle-class man, I could pursue my dream of travelling, the experiences of which have been laid bare in these pages.

I hope that the readers can read the book, in a perspective as to how if you have a vision of travelling the world, it can be accomplished, even with a minimum resource.

<u>INTRODUCTION:</u>

Even though I lived in a small town like Rourkela, I always dreamt of going abroad, which was quite unusual for kids my age. The small city of Rourkela is surrounded by dense jungle, mountains, river Koel and Brahmani, the blue sky and the horizon always fascinated me. My curiosity lay on what was beyond that horizon.

Games like cricket were a bit of luxury back then. I started playing games like "Gulli Danda" and "Pithoo". A few years later, my father bought a football for me. It was the one with a bladder and after inflating it, the stem of the bladder is required to be tied up properly and inserted inside the mouth of the leather football. Finally, the lace was required to be wound. Making the football ready to play with friends was more fun than actually playing the game. My childhood friend Deepak recapitulate those good old memories and we laugh and cherish, several times even today When I went to high school, I started playing basketball and badminton. During our time, matriculation was up to the 11th grade after which I did a year of Pre-University in Government College at Rourkela.

Right from my childhood, the inner fire was always calling me to join the best Engineering college in my state, which was Regional Engineering College, Rourkela. Always seeing the smart students of REC and getting the movie ticket without even standing in the queue was the in thing, which further triggered me to join REC. As, I have mentioned, the first integrated public sector steel plant, was built at Rourkela and it became the first steel city in Odisha. The Graduate Engineering Trainees (GTs) of Rourkela Steel Plant, having the Yezdi motorcycle and driving in the beautiful black pitch ring road further fascinated me to join as GT after passing out from REC (Presently, National Institute of Technology, Rourkela). Eventually, being a fairly good student, I got into REC, Rourkela in 1975 and opted to study Mechanical Engineering as it was the most preferred branch at that time. My branch of choice i.e., Mechanical, out of the 5 branches available was given to me, because of the good marks I had secured in Pre-University. During those days' entrance examination was not conducted to get into REC and our engineering course was of 5 years.

The ultimate aim was to study Engineering, have all types of fun, and at the same time pass Engineering in the final year with reasonably good marks. I must confess, I was not one of the toppers but I passed my Mechanical Engineering with more than 70% marks which was extremely satisfying for me. Then to fulfil my dream, I wanted to join the Rourkela Steel Plant as a GT (Graduate Trainee). Subsequently, when our batch graduated from REC, the name was changed from GT to MT(T) i.e., Management Trainee (Technical). My sole aim was to become a MT(T) so that I can fulfil my dreams of buying first, a Yezdi motorcycle, a camera, and a good music system.

Probably, that was my ultimate dream, but at the back of my mind, something else was always hitting me. Another dream that was beyond my comprehension, something truly grand. The dream that I had as a child of knowing what's beyond the horizon. How did Europe and the USA look like?? How does one go there? And so on…

Table of Contents

Chapter 1:

<u>The Yezdi, the tea kiosk, and a vanity case</u>

After graduating from Regional Engineering College, Rourkela in 1980, I got selected as a Management Trainee(Technical) in SAIL and got posted at the Bokaro Steel Plant. The posting at Bokaro made me very sad, for two reasons. Firstly, I was born and brought up in Rourkela and could never imagine being posted somewhere else, other than Rourkela Steel Plant. Secondly, all my close friends were posted at RSP. However, I joined Bokaro on 19th November 1980 as an MT(T) and started staying at Sector-3 trainees' hostel. After training, I was posted at a department named Coke Ovens, which further frustrated me and I kept thinking of how to come back to the Rourkela Steel Plant. The Coke Oven Department was the farthest department from the main gate and hence it was difficult for me to commute such a distance with an old bicycle which I used during my college days. My father rode the same bi-cycle during his early days. Sometimes I used to take a lift to my department and would often be late, because of all these reasons.

As I was interested in Photography as well, I first bought a camera. The cost of the camera was around Rs1500/- (Rupees fifteen hundred only). I started taking random photographs with my friends at Bokaro and even in the park with the black and white image in that camera, as the coloured film was not available at that time in Bokaro.

But that was not the end of my desires and dreams. One fine morning I wrote a letter to my father, that unless I have a Yezdi motorcycle, I couldn't go to my department every day. I would like to resign from my job if this ordeal continues. I received a letter from my father within 7 days that he would be sending some money for the motorcycle and that I should arrange for the rest of the cost. That day was one of the most exciting days for me and I celebrated it with my friends, but was thinking, how to save balance money for the bike when my total salary was Rs.750/- per month. The cost of the Yezdi motorcycle was Rs. 11,300/- at that time. I was required to save some money which was deficit of my father's contribution towards the motorcycle. Saving that balance amount also seemed like a herculean task for me. The very next month, we had a salary hike and we started getting Rs 1100/- per month, which was big relief for me. With extreme difficulty, I could save some money within 3 months for my motorcycle's initial deposit. Thereafter I had to wait for 2 months to get the bike because of a long waiting queue. Finally, I got my bike in August 1981. I was in seventh heaven, riding a new bike. My eldest brother, who is a doctor, got married in February 1982 and with one of my friends, Ravi, I came to Rourkela for the wedding, on my Yezdi motorcycle from Bokaro. Ravi was staying with his sister & brother-in-law at Bokaro. Without informing them, we started from Bokaro at 6 in the morning and came via, Ramgarh, Ranchi, Gumla, Simdega, and Biramitrapur. Incidentally, Ravi's elder brother was staying at Biramitapur. Since it was late winter and by the time, we reached Biramitrapur, it was 6 PM and became totally dark, we decided to stay back at Ravi's brother house. His brother took us to the club and it was a great experience to see the old British style club and have food in the beautiful ambience of the club. The next morning, we started from Biramitrapur and reached Rourkela safely.

It was a nice memory with my friend Ravi and the long ride in the new Yezdi motorcycle. However, my desire to come back to Rourkela was not dampened. Finally, I came back to Rourkela Steel Plant, with lot of effort, in the month of October 1982. i.e., after almost 2 years. I was extremely thrilled after my transfer. I was posted in a department called Blooming and slabbing mill at RSP. I started coming in shift duty and continued the shift up to April 1986. In the meantime, I was transferred to the Electrical sheet mill in 1986 and I still continued my shift duty up to 1989.

The excitement of coming back to Rourkela in 1982 and spending good times with my old friends fascinated me more. One evening, I along with two of my friends Ajodhya, Sudhanshu were spending time in a tea kiosk in a marketplace called "Ambagan" where, we were chit-chatting. A brilliant idea came to one of my friends- a trip to Goa. Immediately we agreed and planned the trip.

It was the month of February 1983 that we went to Bombay by train and reached the Victoria Terminus (VT) station. We went straight to Navy Nagar, Colaba, and stayed with our friend who was a commissioned officer with the Indian Navy. The location was by the side of the sea and was extremely beautiful. Eating in the command mess was a unique experience as you get alcohol and food both at a very low price. The etiquette maintained inside the command mess was different than our normal eating lifestyle. We were eating with spoon, a fork and a knife and after finishing the food, one was required to keep the fork and knife in tilted and crossed position over the plate. That indicated that one has completed eating. Our friend in Navy, once took us to an eating joint called 'Dilli Darbar' in Kolaba, where they served 'Dabba gosth' which was just awesome. We went to that joint 2 to 3 times during our total stay of 4 days. Every evening we spent time in the marine drive and had ice cream in a parlour called 'Yankee Doodles'. Perched in a 'Tanga' we enjoyed the view of the 'Queen's Necklace' which is the reflection of the street lights in the curved road of the Marine drive in the water of the sea.

Another area of enjoyment was the Gateway of India and traveling in a steamer in the sea and looking at the view of Legendary hotel Taj

Mahal and Taj Intercontinental. These are some of the experiences in Bombay on our debut visit in February 1983.

From Bombay, we travelled to Goa overnight by bus and reached around at 7 in the morning. The moment we got down in Panjim City bus-stand at Goa, we met one smart gentleman, who introduced himself as Mr. Lobo and a local. Since we were young, without thinking him to be a stranger we took his help and advice. We went to a Hotel near Miramar beach named 'Hotel Delmon' as recommended by Mr. Lobo. He gave us several unique tips, how to enjoy Goa. Every evening, we went to a hotel called 'Hotel London' where we had dinner because the main attraction was the 'Live Band'. Every day we enjoyed the live band, the food with some drinks.

We went on tour to both north and south Goa and visited almost all the beaches. One of the major attractions near our hotel was Miramar beach and the "Dona Paula" at River Zuari. Another day we went to Anjuna beach. From there, we walked along the beach, more than 2 km, and saw something very astonishing. Hundreds of foreign tourists were lying on the sea beach, almost nude. As suggested by Mr. Lobo, we enjoyed bathing in the sea, without disturbing them. We spent the whole day on the sea beach and developed friendships with a few of them. That day, we survived on beer and fruits alone, which was being sold by female hawkers, who were local Goans. Such memories of Goa are engraved and alive in me even today. After 4 days of a fun-filled stay in Goa, we returned to Bombay by ship on the upper deck. The first 3 hours' journey on a ship in the deep sea was a new experience and very enjoyable. All the three of us were Engineers and preferred to see the engine room. I along with another friend talked to the captain of the ship and saw the engine from an engineer's perspective, which was nice and a different experience.

But, at the same time, I was always thinking about my abroad trip and my urge to go abroad was not dampened, even after the enjoyable

Goa trip. After a couple of months, after a bit fading of nostalgia of Goa, again, we were sitting in the same tea kiosk and decided to go to Kathmandu, Nepal. Our excitement started, just after discussion and it was at the beginning of September 1984, that we went to Kathmandu. During this visit along with Sudhanshu,Ajodhya and I ,another childhood friend Tulsi, joined us.

The feeling of going abroad was an amazing one. But we did not have much money to fly from Kolkata to Kathmandu (Nepal). The only airline, which was flying then from Kolkata was "Royal Nepal Air Lines". We chose to go by train from Rourkela. We were wondering and getting excited about how to reach Kathmandu. From Rourkela, we went to Jamshedpur (TATA) and from there we went to Patna. In Patna, we stayed in a hotel for two days and visited different parts of Patna including the river Ganga and "Golghar". In the evening, we saw a movie titled "Aaj Ki Awaaz" featuring Nana Patekar, Raj Babbar, and Smita Patil in a nice theatre hall. The next morning, from Patna, we started for Raksaul by bus. It was at the border of Bihar and India. We then crossed the border of India and through the check gate, we walked through Birgang, which is the border of Nepal. During, those days no passport or visa was required to go to Nepal. Since, we could not get a bus at night, as one of the bridges leading to Kathmandu had collapsed, we stayed back in a small hotel at the border in Birgang. The next morning, we started again by bus to Kathmandu. Around 5 in the evening we reached and checked in a hotel at the heart of the city.

We asked the reception, about food and drink etc. in Kathmandu, as that was a very important aspect for us. The man in the reception could understand and replied "You can get good food and drinks, Sir" and he suggested we have "Khukri Rum". We had that rum sometimes, with food in the cold climate of Nepal. The very day that we reached Kathmandu, we discovered from the hotel that there is a complimentary bus service to the only Casino in Kathmandu, named

'Casino Nepal'. The four of us boarded the bus from a nearby square operated by the hotel that was operating the Casino. The hotel was operated by the Oberois and the name of the hotel was 'Soaltee Oberoi". We had a lot of apprehension in our minds as it was our first experience getting into a casino. A complimentary 30ml Johnnie Walker Red Label whisky was being served there. Among four of us, our friend Ajodhya was a teetotaller. So, I took his quota also and my free drink amounted to 60ml. Then we started playing in the 'Money machine". It was very exciting and we won money in the beginning and finally, all of us lost some amount of money. Then we entered further inside and found hundreds of people playing Roulette with a lot of ladies around. We never had such an experience and we did not play anything as we did not have sufficient money and found it to be risky for people like us. We came out and preferred to have street food, which was very enjoyable. Around midnight we reached our hotel.

The next day we went for a city tour, organised by our hotel by a taxi. At Kathmandu all taxis were Toyotas. We had a great time travelling the whole day in that Toyota, as in India, at that time only Ambassador and Fiat cars were plying as taxi. We went to the world-famous 'Pashupatinath Temple". We had a real pious feeling at the temple. After developing a friendship with the driver of the taxi and knowing about several places to visit, our driver strongly recommended us to go to 'Nagarkot'. We also agreed to his proposal and decided to go. That place is an army base of Nepal and the main attraction of the place is the sunrise at the backdrop of Mount Everest. Four of us started at around 4 AM in the Toyota and reached the spot around 5 AM. The drive through the mountainous terrain for more than an hour was a unique experience. Nagarkot was situated at +15,000 ft. from the Mean Sea Level. It was extremely cold and full of clouds passing through all around us superficially. Everything else was almost invisible. We stood on the top of the mountain anxiously waiting to see the sunrise at the backdrop of Mount Everest. Finally, the long awaiting sight was visible and we all were in our seventh heaven seeing the breath-taking sight. After, Nagarkot visit, we returned to the hotel. That day, we kept our programme for shopping and also went to the Tibet market. The next day we had a plan to go to 'Pokhra', but due to heavy rain, we could not make it.

Thereafter, we did not have any other plan to go anywhere else and thought to leave Kathmandu. The same evening, that we stayed back in our room due to rain, we started having "Khukri Rum". After having a couple of rum, we suddenly decided to go to Darjeeling. We did not even know the route to go to Darjeeling from Kathmandu and on inquiry, we could find that the best way is to go to Kakadbhitta by bus from Kathmandu. Kakadbhitta is on the border of Nepal and by crossing the border, the Indian side of the border was Naxalbari, which is situated in Siliguri of West Bengal. We boarded the bus from Kathmandu at around 9 pm. It was a 40-seater bus and the headroom was very less. The distance from Kathmandu to Kakadbhitta was around 460km and it was a very difficult terrain. The driver of the bus said it would take around 10 to 11 hours, but though we started around 9 pm, after 3 hours of drive, the driver went for food and did not come back for 3 hours. Many of us searched for him but could discover that after food, he was gambling. There was a lot of hues and cry and finally, the bus started at around 3:30 in the morning. We reached Kakadbitta around 11. 30am. We were extremely tired and crossing the border was a big hassle. I had my old camera, which was required to be produced at the check gate along with other articles that we brought from Kathmandu. The brokers were badly after us thinking that we have lots of articles and money and prompted us to take their help in crossing the border. We were all a bit scared and tired too. Finally, we crossed the border by walking through the check gate, without taking any help from the brokers. However, crossing the border and reaching Naxalbari was a big relief for us. We then hired an auto rickshaw and came to the Siliguri bus stand. It took around an hour and we were famished by that time. We had our food and decided to hire a taxi and straight go to Darjeeling to reach early. The driver took us to one of the hotels named "Hotel Purnima". It was the month of September, when we reached Dargiling and the next month was Durga Puja. Normally, the rush starts during Durga puja holidays and we had arrived much earlier. Hence, getting a hotel was not a problem for us. We bargained and got a good deal as it was a lean season, and stayed in Hotel Purnima. By then it was evening and we asked for a good drink and some food. The hotel boy recommended 'Fireball brandy' along with food. We ordered one bottle of Fireball brandy which was an apple-shaped red bottle and the taste was awesome. Our hotel was uphill and there was a terrace from where the Kanchenjunga range was visible. The view of the snow-peak mountain range was extremely beautiful.

As usual, we enquired in the hotel and the next day, hired a jeep for the tour. We visited several places including Cactus Garden, Sherpa Mountaineering School, and the famous Mirik Lake. The fishes in the lake were jumping, which was a beautiful sight. On the third day one of our friends fell sick and was down with a fever. We took him to a doctor. The doctor after inquiry diagnosed him with 'high altitude sickness' and said he would be fine within 2 days, but should not travel. That particular day we did not travel anywhere and relaxed in the hotel, enjoying the beauty of Kanchenjunga from the terrace. After spending one more day we came to New Jalpaiguri station and boarded 'Kanchanjanga Express' for Kolkata. During those days the reservation was a very big issue and we were young enough not to bother about the reservation on the train. We travelled in the unreserved third-class compartment and reached Sialdah station. We could see the Farraka Dam on the way, which was a nice scene. After reaching Sialdah, we came to Howrah station to board our home-bound train to Rourkela. That is how my debut visits abroad came to an end with a lot of beautiful memories.

Thereafter, in the same year in 1984, I was very fortunate enough to get married. On 26th November I got married, and again, I and my wife Rachita travelled to Goa in December 1984, for our honeymoon. I had saved some money exclusively for this trip. I had a lot of good experiences in Goa and took my wife to some good places, as I had seen the places earlier. Of course, we went first to Mumbai and stayed there with one of my distant relatives. They received us from the station and treated us with the utmost kindness. But then, we did not have the freedom of freak out, which one would have done on a honeymoon trip. However, the next day itself we decided to go to Goa and have fun there. We promised our relatives that we would stay with them on our return journey.

We had an overnight journey to Goa from Mumbai by bus and had a beautiful experience. As, I had travelled in the ship, with my friends from Goa to Bombay in 1983, we had seen all the facilities in the ship. The ship also had beautiful cabins on the top floor. I had a dream of coming in the cabin with my wife, from Goa to Bombay. When I enquired at the reception of the hotel in Goa, to book a cabin for my return journey, they tried and failed. Finally, the proprietor of the hotel asked for my service identity card for booking the cabin in the ship if I am an executive of the government of India or PSU, for which there was one reserved cabin. Unfortunately, I had not carried my Identity card and therefore could not produce it. All this fiasco led to nothing and I could not get the cabin ticket. Probably, that was a boon in disguise. I had never travelled in an aeroplane until then, and the inner desire again prevailed. I asked at the hotel, how much would the flight ticket cost from Goa to Bombay. He enquired and replied, it is Rs.365/- (Rupees three hundred sixty-five only). I decided to fly from Goa to Bombay, which my wife was dead against, thinking that we would spend too much money and my parents (Her in-laws) may not like that. But I insisted and we came by flight. It was my debut travel by flight and the experience of travelling by aeroplane was extremely amazing.

But then, everything does not go smoothly all the time. After we landed in Mumbai, we boarded a taxi from the airport and came to Sivaji Park. There was a nice system in vogue at the airport. The name of the passenger and the number of the taxi along with the name of the driver was being recorded in a register. When we reached Sivaji Park, where we were putting up, we unloaded all the luggage from the taxi. While going to the 1st floor by stairs, Rachita suddenly started screaming, saying that, she left her 'Vanity case' in the taxi and she started crying. I asked her to go home and I would look into the matter. By the time I came to the road, the taxi had already left. I was a bit puzzled and could not understand for a moment, "What to do??". I got reminded of the data entry by the airport police at the airport regarding the taxi and passenger. Immediately, I rushed to the airport by another taxi and enquired about the taxi that we had boarded. I could get all details from the counter at the airport. They suggested I go to the airport police station to lodge a complaint. I immediately went to the airport police station and asked for help. I was very nervous, which the police officer could sense. He looked very smart yet aggressive, at the same time, he was very courteous. He offered me a chair, a glass of water and asked me to write a complaint (FIR). I did that and he assured me of getting the Vanity case back, but it may take some time.

With a gloomy face, I came back to Sivaji Park. I narrated the whole story to Mrs. & Mr. Bhat, with whom we were staying. Mr. Bhat took all the details from me and assured us that he will do his best. We then got a bit relaxed and took a rest in the afternoon. In the evening, Rachita and I went for dinner to a beautiful restaurant nearby. The ambiance and atmosphere were very cosy. We did not discuss anything about the morning episode and wanted to relax. But at the back of our mind that episode was repeatedly coming and we were bit upset. The next day; Mrs. & Mr. Bhat also took us for dinner to Juhu. We had a good time at Juhu beach and then had our dinner with them.

The next day, we came back to Rourkela by a train named Bombay-Howrah Express. As usual, the return journey was a bit sad, as our holiday and the honeymoon trip were coming to an end. At the same time, Rachita was very apprehensive of two things. First, we had travelled by aeroplane from Goa to Bombay, which of course, I had forced her and secondly, she had lost her vanity case. She didn't know how she would face my parents. We reached home after a day and a half and my parents were overwhelmed to see us after a long time. They were, in fact, happy that we had travelled by aeroplane from Goa to Bombay. About the vanity case, Rachita revealed it the next day, but to our surprise, after narrating the truth, they appreciated and assured us of getting back the vanity case. Just after 4 weeks, I got a letter from Mr. Bhat that the vanity case has been located and the police wanted an authorisation letter to hand over the case to Mr. Bhat. The very day I sent an authorisation letter and Mr. Bhat got back the case from the police. Mr. Bhat sent the case from Bombay and after two days we received the case at Rourkela, When Rachita opened the case, it was miraculous to see that, all articles in the case were intact, including Rs.800/-, which she had kept in the case and even had not revealed to me.

After a long holiday, I joined my office at end of December 1984 and had the same routine life of the Steel Plant. During those days, once a month, we visited a restaurant named 'Maurya' for dinner. I still remember, at that time a slogan was displayed in front of the restaurant "Drop in at any time". The restaurant was specialised in north Indian food. During those days, Ghazal was the new craze. The Ghazal of Pankaj Udhas, "Pio Lekin Rakho Hisab" was being played in that restaurant. Those were the unforgettable little moments of our newly married life.

Chapter 2:

Large Pizzas; Larger Airports

We were blessed with a daughter in November 1985 following which eating out and travelling were on hold for more than a year. However, responsibilities increased after having a baby, and as such availability of disposable money for travelling was inadequate. Hence travelling got curtailed to a great extent. Nevertheless, it did not stop completely, and we travelled to some places within India. Our second daughter was born in 1991 and our responsibilities increased further. But then I was waiting for a visit to Europe and it was just not possible, with the kind of salary that I was getting. The only possibility of a trip to Europe was, if it would be sponsored by my company 'Rourkela Steel Plant, SAIL'.

At the back of my mind, it was always hitting me, how to go to Europe and also USA, as it was my ultimate dream. I chose to change my department to Projects & Modernisation, for which I had to sit for an interview and got selected. During that period the New Continuous Casting Project was coming at Steel Melting Shop-II, which was a new technology for RSP. The Technology provider was M/s Mannesmann Demag, Germany. That project was a very prestigious project for Rourkela Steel Plant. I was fortunately transferred to that particular Project in February 1991. I was extremely happy to get such a prestigious project posting, as there was a ray of hope of going abroad which would be sponsored by my company.

I started thinking, how will I get a chance to go to Germany as soon as possible, sponsored by my company as the collaborating company was

Mannesmann Demag, Germany. After having worked on that project for about 5 years, I finally got selected in 1996, to be trained in Germany and Netherlands for 4 weeks. It was the month of July and I got a call from my Executive Director (Projects) that I have been chosen for training abroad. I remember vividly that I was in seventh heaven, after getting the information and I rushed to get the copy of the order. There were 4 members in my team, including me. I thanked my Executive Director (Projects) for having chosen me to be trained abroad. After getting the order, I came from the plant to my house and touched the feet of my mother, and hugged her. She was extremely happy, for which I was longing for a very long time, and that had become the only aim of life. I did not even have a passport. Our HRD department made all arrangements and we had a detailed discussion with our travel agent M/s Arya Travels. During those days, we had the option to choose our itinerary fitting into the actual training duration in Germany and Netherlands. We chose to go to Paris and on our return journey via London. Everything was agreed upon by our travel agent. Finally, in July 1996, we got our visa for France, Germany, and the Netherlands. In fact, we were allowed to go to all the 3 countries with one visa. But for London, the VISA requirement was different and UK visa was separately done by our travel agent.

We first proceeded to Calcutta (Now Kolkata) by Shatabdi Express and reached in the evening. We stayed in Park hotel at Calcutta and had a nice experience. The next morning, we were issued US Dollars for our expenses and all flight tickets were delivered to us. First, we flew from Calcutta to Delhi and again stayed there in a 5-star hotel. Those were the days, when I had the first opportunity of staying in any 5-star hotel, as I had never stayed before. Our flight to Paris was at 1am in the morning by Air India. We chose to take 'Smoking seats' and accordingly, all four of us got beautiful seats. The aircraft was a Boeing

747 and the best part was that 40% of seats were empty. It was my first experience travelling in an international carrier. The Air hostess took special care of us and we got Black Label whisky with cashew nut fry. We had a couple of drinks and real fun inside the aircraft. Then we slept for about 2 hours and by then the announcement came that we would be reaching Paris on schedule at 7 in the morning (Paris time). In fact, the travel time was around 8 hours and even with drowsy eyes, our excitement prevailed. We opened our window shields and saw the beautiful clouds. When the aircraft was preparing for the landing, we got a fantastic aerial view of the city of Paris. We landed at Charles de Gaulle Airport, Paris. It was beyond my comprehension, that the airport could be so big and figuratively a madhouse. However, that being our debut visit, we were enquired upon in every stage and passed the immigration and customs. Then we were relaxed and I was not able to internalise the fact that I have landed in Paris. I immediately bought a calling card and from the airport itself, I talked to my mother in India. She was overwhelmed and blessed me, and said: "Your dream has come true". That was the nicest moment of my life.

From the airport, we boarded a bus provided by the airport free of cost and went to our hotel named 'The Novotel'. We took a rest for two hours, freshened up, and went to the breakfast hall. The breakfast was not of our choice as it was full of only salad in the morning. However, we ate, whatever was possible, and went to the reception to enquire about the Paris city tour. The receptionist advised us to book a cab, as there were 4 of us and could be accommodated in one taxi. We did exactly as we were advised and booked a taxi. The driver came around 2 pm with a Toyota car. The driver was very smart carrying a cell phone. Way back in 1996, he was carrying a cell phone which surprised us to a great extent. We first went to the War Memorial area named 'Triumph Arch'. The area is also called the 'Champs Elysees' war memorial. The gigantic 1.9 km long and 70 metres wide Champs Elysees is widely regarded to be one of the most recognisable venues in the world. We spent some time walking through the street and enjoyed the French architecture as well. We then proceeded to Louvre Museum and wanted to see the world-famous 'Monalisa' painting. We got flabbergasted to see thousands of people standing in the queue at the entrance of the museum and could not venture going inside the museum due to paucity of time. However, seeing Louvre from outside and taking photographs with friends, from different angles, was a great experience. Our next visiting place was the iconic Eiffel tower, which we had read about and heard from many. The temptation to reach that area itself was giving us immense pleasure. Even from a distance, we could see the glimpse of the Eiffel Tower and our driver was giving us running commentary in English about the places. At that time, it was around 5 pm and we decided to relax in the garden area having beautiful lawns and water fountains. I and one of my friends, Subrat Sen went in search of beer. We got it from one of the kiosks and started having a beer. We saw something very typical that young boys and girls were skating with one leg roller skating, that was a unique visual. Many young ones were bathing in the pool and water fountains. Having seen all these and experiencing it was absolutely new for us.

We were waiting for the sun to set so that we could go to the top of the Eiffel tower. That being the month of July, we knew that sunset would be around 9:30 pm, and we had sufficient time in hand. My friend and I went again to bring a few more cans of beer and kept 2 cans reserved to have it at the top of the Eiffel tower. Around 7.30 pm we decided to climb the Eiffel tower. Out of the 4 of us, only three decided to climb to the topmost floor which is at a height of 276 metres (the height of the Eiffel tower is 300 metres). But our friend

Raja opted to drop out to go to the top. We bought the tickets and went by the lift to the 1st floor initially. Then we further went to the 3rd floor, also by lift, which was the topmost floor. When we reached the top floor, the sun had not set yet and it was an amazing sight, standing on the top floor of Eiffel tower and getting the entire view of Paris. At that unforgettable moment, the beer cans we carried were of great use. Out of the 3 of us, I and my friend Subrat Sen were the drinkers. We had the beer that we carried at that height of the tower. The breeze was enchanting and having beer further enhanced our thrill. Gradually, the sun started setting and the whole of Paris city started glowing with beautiful lights. Lighting started in the tower itself, which of course we could not visualise suddenly. Our driver was not only a driver but also a perfect guide. He had said, once we get down from the Eiffel tower, we must travel on a cruise in the river Seine. All of us got down from the tower and our lone friend Raja who did not climb was anxiously waiting downstairs for us. We did not have any mode of communication to tell Raja and though angry, he did not have any choice, but to wait on the ground at a spot, near Eiffel tower as decided before climbing the tower.

All four of us, then went on the cruise. There was a provision of food and beverage on the cruise and the travel time was about an hour. Travelling on the cruise with the dining and beer was truly amazing. The best scene that we could enjoy in the river Seine from the cruise were the lights on the Eiffel tower. The lights were changing frequently and it was unique from different angles while moving on the cruise. We then came back to the land again and by then it was around 10:30 pm and we were feeling hungry. All of us decided to have street food with a beautiful ambience, full of lights all around. There were several counters and the area was crowded and very lively. We saw pizzas of around 800mm to 1m in diameter and were surprised. Raja, who did not climb the Eiffel tower was a vegetarian and it was very difficult to get a veg pizza for him. He chose to eat fruits instead. But the rest of us wanted to have a bite of the pizza which was again available in different varieties. Pizza with pork, beef, lamb, and chicken. We had the chicken pizza and it was a lifetime experience, as, first of all, I had never tasted such a pizza, and secondly the size of the pizza was huge. By the time we finished eating our pizza, it was midnight, which we had not realised as were lost in oblivion. Suddenly, we realised that our flight to Dusseldorf, Germany, was on the next day at 11 am. Our cab driver also dined with us and he never disturbed us or reminded us of being late, as he was enjoying our childlike behaviour. We then boarded the taxi and reached our hotel around 1 am. We thanked the driver for being very nice and patient with us.

The next day, before 9 am we rushed to the Charles de Gaulle Airport by the shuttle bus service and after finishing all formalities, we boarded the flight around 10:30 am. The flight was Air France and it was an Airbus 320. While travelling from Delhi to Paris by Air India, around 30-35% of the passengers were Indians, but in the flight from Paris to Dusseldorf, the four of us were the only Indian passengers. The rest of them were all either Germans or from other parts of the world. The travelling time was only about 1 hour and we reached Dusseldorf airport around 12 noon. To our surprise, at that time the airport was in shambles as a major fire had occurred in Dusseldorf airport in April of the same year. When we landed there in July, the catastrophe could be vividly felt. However, our baggage came in small belts in an open yard, and there we met my nephew Sukant, who was working as a Security Officer in the Airport. Though I had contacted him earlier and had said about our programme, I had never expected that he would be available at the airport. He helped us a lot and it was very nostalgic to meet him in a foreign land. We then came outside the airport and found a driver wearing a suit with a plaque card in his hand. The vehicle was a big Mercedes SUV. The driver was very cautious and took us to Duisburg, where the head office of M/s Mannesmann Demag was situated. We reached Duisburg within 45 minutes. The drive was a great experience and we directly went to the hotel named 'Hotel Konti'. It was a family-managed, beautiful, and cosy hotel. The rooms were very airy, well-lighted, and spacious. The season being July, there were a lot of flowers which we could see all around. The hotel building was so designed that just outside the window panes, there were inbuilt flower pots and all the pots were full of flower plants like pansies, petunias, etc. It was in its full bloom and the whole building with those flowers was looking amazing. It was a unique sight for us. We took a rest and then had lunch. That being a Sunday, roads were not crowded. We walked through the streets and enjoyed the breeze and the sight of the beautiful clean & blue sky. Ours is a tropical country, we were habituated to a bit hazy atmosphere and that is the reason why the blue and clean sky fascinated us. On the top of it, on most of the buildings, the window area was full of flowers, similar to that of our hotel. That was truly a new experience for us.

After an hour or so, we decided to go to a nearby town and discovered 'Dortmund' on the map. We travelled by local train and reached Dortmund. The high-speed train took hardly about 40 minutes to reach Dortmund. We travelled around the city and at around 7 pm came back to Duisburg. The next day being Monday and the first day of our theoretical training, we had our dinner a bit early and slept. The next day, a vehicle came for us around 9:30 am, which was communicated to us earlier, sent by M/s Mannesmann Demag. We were absolutely ready to go to the office for training. But, before that, if I don't describe the breakfast, it would not be proper and complete. It was a hot breakfast with all possible types of bread, dry fruits, juices, and several types of even mineral water. We tried most of them and I must say, after having a typical breakfast with only salad in the morning at hotel Novotel, in Paris, it was a lifetime experience here, having such a sumptuous breakfast.

We reached the head office of M/s Mannesmann Demag and were escorted to the Training Centre. We had the introductory session and were given several coupons including money (Deutschmark) as per the contract. Euro was not introduced during those days. Further, we were provided with lunch in the office canteen every day except Saturday and Sunday. Our company had a full-fledged written contract agreement with the German counterpart and accordingly our training coordinator disbursed Deutschmark for our expenses. The weekends used to be very exciting as we were getting direct cash in Deutschmark in addition to our US Dollar which was given to us by our company, before we travelled to Germany.

The office canteen that we used to have lunch was huge and had a variety of food and beverages including ice cream. The first 2 days we enjoyed the food in the canteen with the flavour of smoked Salmon fish and then we became very selective in eating. Some evenings our coordinator took us to a restaurant for dinner. He also took us even to Indian restaurants in the week ends, along with his colleagues. Though we were in our late thirties, but our instructor was in his late fifties and still, he was very sportive and cooperative too. Every day our training used to be over by 5 pm and then we were free. We spent our time in big departmental stores which was a new experience for us and it was a shopping spree, that being my debut visit to Europe and that too Germany. One evening, our coordinator invited us to have a beer and took us to a brewery. That was the first time that I had the experience of having a beer in a brewery, having large copper containers with copper piping. Several varieties of fresh draught beer were available and we had a couple of them with different snacks.

On Tuesday afternoon, a German lady called me while our classroom training was in progress. It was a bit of a surprise for me, but I had some clue. She was the wife of my nephew, Sukant, whom I had met in the Dusseldorf airport. She was a German lady and was working in that office at Duisburg. She invited for dinner to their house at Dusseldorf, where they were living. I accepted the invitation. The next day being Wednesday, I went to Sukant's house along with his wife, directly from the office around 5:15 pm. We reached around 6 pm at their house at Dusseldorf and I got a very warm welcome from both Sukant and his wife. Talking to Sukant in our language and dialect was fun. His wife was not understanding anything and we would explain to her, what we were talking about. Then we decided to start a conversation only in English which she knew quite well.

By around 6:45 pm, they first offered me a sparkling white wine with some dry snacks and it was amazing. After having 2 glasses of wine, Sukant offered me 'Jack Daniel' whisky with a lamb chop and a lot of salad. It was just awesome. After having a couple of drinks, we sat for the main course dinner. I was surprised, that he was continuously offering one thing or the other. We had chicken and many other dishes followed by ice cream. The food was a bit heavy for me and then finally Sukant said, with this kind of full 3-course dinner, the evening would be incomplete without Cognac. During those days, I didn't know much about Cognac and of course, knew about Wine and Whisky. He said, after having food, we would have 'Remy Martin, VSOP' cognac, and the next morning, everything would get digested and I would feel fresh. He offered me the Remy Martin VSOP on the rocks and that was the finale. Then both Sukant and his wife, who drove the car, dropped me at my hotel in Duisburg. It was a truly an unforgettable evening of my life.

The next day, as usual, we had our training session and, in the evening, again, we moved around the streets in the market area of Duisburg. On Thursday afternoon, we requested our coordinator to excuse us for some time for shopping and to visit the Duisburg Zoo. Just after lunch, we started for the world-famous Duisburg Zoo, where the biggest attraction was the dolphin and whale show. It was one of its kind and I saw it for the first time in my life. The dolphin show was inside a pond which was covered and surrounded by a gallery for the spectators. One man was playing with 5 dolphins, which was just amazing. Even the whale show was something, beyond my comprehension. We then proceeded to a market, which was famous for house appliances and garden equipment. As I knew that my father was a great lover of gardens and gardening, I bought a grafting knife, an inarching knife, hand gloves, rose cutter, etc., for him.

The next day was a Friday and in the second half, we were given some German Currency Deutschmark, as per the contract agreement. We were also given train & cruise coupons by our coordinator. It was a great and pleasant surprise for us. We were given some tips and some travel plans to travel in a cruise in river Rhine. That evening was a very exciting evening for us and we made a detailed plan for the next day, by seeing the map of the area.

The next morning, we got up early and started around 8 am from Duisburg by train to Cologne which is not only a tourist spot but also a very ancient and one of the largest cities of Germany. The landmark church of Cologne called 'Cologne Cathedral', the tallest twin-spired church in the world, is unique in the sense that it is not possible to take the full photograph of the church from the front angle. It was an ancient Roman Catholic church with beautiful architecture. We spent about an hour in the church and then went to see the rest of the city. Our prime objective was to travel by cruise in the River Rhine, for which we had pre-booked tickets. From Cologne, we went to a place called Koblenz by train. It was a beautiful small town in Germany, from where our cruise was supposed to start. We went to the riverside of Koblenz and by then it was around noon and it was a pleasant sunny day. We were feeling hungry and there was only a small kiosk near the riverside, where we had hamburgers and immediately boarded the cruise. It was a huge cruise & food and drink were abundantly available inside. Our cruise tour was from South to North. It was a narrated sightseeing tour on the cruise that lasted for more than 2 hours. The scenic panorama of the majestic castles, churches, and vineyards along the bank of Rhine was just amazing. The forested hills, rugged cliffs, and terraced vineyards as the cruise made its way through some of the country's most dramatic landscapes, were worth the view. On top of it, having different types of snacks with cans of beer in the cruise along with the breeze and listening to the narration, enjoying the panoramic view, just cannot be forgotten.

After having spent the whole day with a different kind of enjoyment, we came back to our hotel at Duisburg around 8 pm. By then, we were tired, and as such our stomach was full. Hence, we slept quite early. The next day we were supposed to go to the Netherlands, as our theoretical training was scheduled for only one week and was over on Friday in Germany. On Sunday morning, we were ready by 10.30 am after packing our bags and baggage. Then, we started for the next destination for our, practical training at Hoogovens, Netherlands. From Duisburg, we started by an SUV and again the driver was English-speaking and smart. Around 10:30 am we started for a place called Katwijk. As promised by the driver, it took us around 2 ½ hours to reach Katwijk. As usual, the roads from Germany to the Netherlands were fantastic and no separate visa was required. Further, no prominently visible border between Germany and Netherland was there. However, we asked our driver to stop at the border to have an experience. The diver did so and we got down at the border of Germany and the Netherlands for about 10 minutes. Both sides were full of greenery and the scenery was beautiful. After we entered Netherland, the driver took us directly to a beach without even informing us. We got down on the beach and enjoyed it for about 20 minutes. Hundreds of people were bathing and sunbathing on the sea beach. It was a unique scene for us. Then around 1:30 pm, we reached the hotel at Katwijk. To our surprise, the hotel was situated by the side of the sea that the driver took us to and it was only a 5 minutes' walk to the beach from our hotel. We were fascinated to get such a nice location for a 3 weeks' stay. Then we went inside the hotel and found that it was a pub attached with hotel rooms, owned by a Dutch family. The owner of the hotel was in his late fifties and was a perfect gentleman. Since it was an afternoon in summer days, the moment we reached the hotel, the owner offered us chilled beer, which we enjoyed, and then we were given the rooms. The rooms were huge with a kitchen facility. On the first day, the owner explained to us about the whole area. In the evening we went to the nearby supermarket and bought all the items required for preparing food in the room. The hotel was serving us complimentary breakfast every day. Of course, the breakfast was not as lavish as in Germany, because there were limited items on the menu.

The day we reached Katwijk was a Sunday, and the next day was our first day of practical training. On Monday morning one smart young gentleman came to our hotel with a big van. He was in fact our training coordinator and arrived in his own van. He took us to the steel plant i.e., Hoogovens, Ijmuiden. The driving time from our hotel to the steel plant was around 45 minutes. On the first day, our coordinator, helped us in getting the gate pass made. He then took us to the old Steel melting shop and introduced us to all the executives of the department. We again had our department visits and some theoretical training up to Friday. We were further left with 2 more weeks for the training. We were asked to come in shift duty in groups. As instructed, the four of us got divided into two groups each. My roommate Subrat and I chose to be in one group. Though initially, we did not like to go on shift duty, after knowing that for every 3 days working in a shift, we would get 2 days off, that was a big surprise and relief. In that process, we would get more time to travel to different parts of the country.

On the weekend of the first week, our coordinator took us to Amsterdam by van. To go to Amsterdam was a dream for us and the commute was only 50 minutes to 1 hour. That element of commuting time gave us further pleasure and confidence that we could visit Amsterdam, of our own again. On that day, we started around 2 pm along with our coordinator and he took us to several visiting places including the boat ride. He also took us to a beautiful restaurant where we had an early dinner and came back to our hotel by 9:30 pm. Still, we had some other places in mind which we could not visit on that day, primarily, the nightclubs, which is a very famous art exhibition in Amsterdam.

The next week, again our coordinator, took us to the famous city, The Hague. On the way, he took us to his village for a cup of coffee. We went to his house and for the first time saw 'community gardening' i.e., in a common piece of land all the residents of the place would be growing their own vegetables and flowers of their choice. Our coordinator's wife was very hospitable and showed us around their house. We were amazed to see such a huge wooden double storied house with slanting tile roof in the countryside. Even the internal roads in such a countryside were unthinkable.

After spending about 30 minutes in their house, we proceeded to The Hague. First, we saw the famous International Court of Justice. Then, he took us to a place 'Madurodam', which was a surprise for us. It was an amazing theme park. It was a miniature park and a tourist attraction in The Hague. It is home to a range of 1:25 scale model replicas of famous Dutch landmarks, historical cities, and large developments. Most of the models were real-animate models and we had never seen such a model park in our life. From there, we went to some of the historical windmills, which are very famous in the Netherlands. It was around a half-hour journey from The Hague, that we reached the windmill. Though the windmill was not in running condition, it was something unique to see. The heavy wooden structure was well maintained and the best part of the windmil was that the basement was converted into a cheese factory. We could see the manufacturing of cheese and the windmill in one place. Near the entrance on the boundary of the windmill, there were a few hawkers. One of our friends, Rizvy, saw some fish and called us. He was a voracious reader and knew about some specialities of the Netherlands. It was a display of Herring fish that were dipped in salt and vinegar water in big jars. He said, he would eat them and ate a few. It was raw, neither fried nor smoked or skewed. But after seeing my friend eating the fish, I also got tempted to eat and ate a few. Though, not very tasty for me, it had a different and typical taste.

After travelling the whole day, we came back to the hotel and slept. It was the third week and we were left with only one week. As usual, we continued our training in shift duty and decided to go to Amsterdam once again, on our own. By then we had a good amount of exposure and experience in the Netherlands. That being the last week of our stay there, the forthcoming Saturday, we were supposed to leave for our return journey. Coincidently, we all had the off-day on Wednesday and left for Amsterdam by 9 am. We reached by 10 am and were mentally prepared to spend the whole day in Amsterdam. We were all hungry and went to a street-side pizza corner. After having the typical big pizza in Paris for the first time, we had developed a good taste of pizza. Hence, 2 of us ordered chicken pizza, one friend ordered mushroom pizza and the 4th person Subrat Sen, went inside, ordered something, and came back. After having the pizza, we were walking through the streets and suddenly Subrat started vomiting. Then, he revealed that he had ordered a beef pizza to have a different experience. Although he ate it, he did not feel comfortable, as none of us were beef eaters. After sitting for some time on the benches by the side of the road, we again proceeded.

We first visited some big shopping malls for 2 purposes. The first, was to use the restroom, as, it was difficult to get a public washroom in Amsterdam during those days, and secondly, we did not know how a big shopping mall looks like. After that, we went to the 'Madam Tussaud's Museum', which was a new experience for us. The statues of top celebrities made from wax were astonishing in that museum. We enjoyed those places and remembered the instruction of our training coordinator. He was always asking us whether we have visited the "Cultural Hub" of the Netherlands, which we understood later, meant the night clubs and the red-light area of Amsterdam. We were curious to see the speciality of that area. We were told to be careful at

Amsterdam of pickpockets, especially in the red-light area. Since we were a group of four, we were always together and were alert. We just walked through the different streets of the red-light area and enjoyed the view. Girls would be standing nude in style inside air-conditioned glass chambers. That was a unique experience for all of us. After, moving in that area for about an hour, we came back and had our lunch in the central market place.

Our next programme was to see the floor show, which is very famous in Amsterdam, as repeatedly recommended by our coordinator. The recommended place was 'Casa Rosso'. Though the entry ticket was very costly, we could not resist ourselves to have the experience of watching the show. It was an hour and a half long show. We were given a complimentary beer along with our entry ticket, following which other drinks were chargeable. The show was nothing but erotic theatre and was unique. We had a lifetime experience watching such a show. After seeing that show, we came to the canal side and travelled in the boat for an hour and enjoyed the evening. We then decided to go back to our hotel. We had our pre-booked ticket in the train and hence travelled by train to our destination Katwijk. That was our last week and we were left with only 2 days for our training. It was a mixed feeling for us, that we were a bit homesick and at the same time, we would be leaving the Netherlands. But then, our silver lining was that we were visiting London, United Kingdom, after that.

After completing 2 more uneventful days of training, on Saturday, we started for Schiphol airport in Amsterdam. It was a beautiful airport and we travelled to London by KLM airlines. The flight took only about an hour and we reached Heathrow airport around noon. It was an amazing experience to land at Heathrow. It was too huge and virtually again a madhouse for us. After immigration, we boarded the shuttle bus to Hotel Ramada, which was booked for us earlier by the travel agent. The hotel was very near to the airport and it took us only 30 minutes to reach the hotel. We received a fantastic reception, in the hotel lobby. The lobby was too huge and full of flower pots. It was an unforgettable and beautiful sight. We were then given individual rooms, which were also very huge and beautiful. The most fascinating event that happened was, the moment I switched on the TV in the room, a message blinked "Welcome Mr. Prabodh Ranjan Padhee, to Hotel Ramada". It touched me and I immediately called and asked my other friends to switch on their TVs. They were also fascinated to see the message addressed to them on the TV. After keeping our luggage in the room and freshening up, we went to the dining hall to have some food. We sat by the side of the window with big glass panes. To our surprise, it was adjacent to the airport and the runway was visible. It was an amazing sight to see the aeroplanes taking off very frequently from one of the busiest airports in the world.

After having some food, we asked at the reception about the travel plan for that day. Our flight back to India was scheduled on Monday, 3 am, London time, and hence, we had sufficient time the next day to travel. As per the tips given in the reception, we went to Piccadilly Circus first. It was a central place in London and very crowded. It is a big marketplace as well. After spending an hour or so, we walked to the Big Ben, Westminster area. The place was beautiful with the breeze blowing through our body, which was further enhancing the excitement. The view of the River Thames was very beautiful from that place. We spent the whole evening in that area and saw the beautiful lighting around us and the reflection of the light on the river. That day we came back to our hotel early and slept. As we had 2 nights stay at London, we had sufficient time in hand to go to other places in London.

The next day, in the morning we came by train again to Piccadilly circus and walked down to Trafalgar square. The pigeons at the Trafalgar square were one of the main attractions. There were thousands of pigeons and the visitors were feeding them with nuts. We also indulged in that activity and enjoyed it thoroughly. We then bought a couple of beer cans and hired an open-top bus to go to Buckingham Palace. There was no restriction to drink beer sitting on the bus. We got down near the palace and walked a bit. It was a beautiful palace, but we were slightly disappointed, as we had seen places like 'Mysore Palace' and 'Taj Mahal', which were not only gigantic but also architecturally much more beautiful as compared to 'Buckingham Palace'. From there we decided again to go to the bank of the River Thames. We spent a few hours in that area and had our food. By then, it was around 4 pm. We boarded a train and came back to our hotel. We relaxed a bit and started packing for our return journey to India. We left just before midnight from our hotel by shuttle, as our return flight was scheduled at 3 am.

We flew back again by Air India and frankly speaking, we were feeling homesick after spending more than a month abroad. As usual, the flight experience was great. My friend Subrat and I, had some complimentary Black Label whisky, and after having a couple of them, we had some food. We might have slept for only 2 hours in the flight, in a total flight duration of about 8 hours. It was a direct flight from London to Delhi and we reached around 8 am at Delhi. After completing all formalities, we came out of the airport around 10:30 am. Though we came through the Green Channel, one of our friends, Rizvy, was asked to open all baggage, which took an additional 30 minutes to come out. We wanted to find out the reason, as to why only that friend was asked to open the bag. However, it was a random checking and we felt relaxed after coming out of the airport and also excited to come back to our homeland after more than a month.

During those days, my sister-in-law, Ishita and co-brother-in-law, Manoj were living in Delhi and they knew about my arrival plan. They were at the hotel, waiting for me. I checked into the hotel near the airport and invited both of them to the room. I then described my experience of the Europe visit and gave them some chocolate and gifts that I had brought for them. They invited me over for lunch. We then proceeded to a nice Mughlai Joint, which they knew quite well. I had Indian beer after about a month and really enjoyed it. The food was also awesome. But the main attraction was, having a betel "Pan' with 'Katha", after a month. Though I was not a regular Pan chewer, I always relished Pan after a sumptuous lunch. Even that day, I enjoyed the pan along with my co-brother-in-law, Manoj. As, our flight from Delhi to Calcutta, was at 5 pm, they dropped me at the hotel and immediately we started for the airport. We reached Calcutta at around 7:30 pm and we went to the hotel named "Hotel Hindustan International". Our scheduled departure of the train was at 7am the next day. We came by Ispat express and reached Rourkela around 2pm. It was such an amazing and thrilling experience to reach home that it cannot be expressed in words. During those days, my father had an Ambassador car, which was waiting for me outside the railway station. My paternal uncle had come to receive me with that car. I was feeling like a VIP and reached home at around 3pm.

Once I reached home, my whole family was in a different state of happiness. My mother hugged me and said, "Your dream of going abroad came true". I remember, vividly, she also said, "I wish and pray, you would be going abroad several times". I was so happy to listen to her blessings. Then, everybody was waiting for me to unpack my suitcases. I brought several gifts and chocolates for every member of my family. Two special gifts were brought by me. One is a big 'Synthesiser' for my elder daughter, who was learning music. The other gift was for my father. The gift for my father was a bit typical, which was only a set of specialised garden equipment like knives, cutters and several types of hand gloves. Those were the costliest gifts, which I brought for my father. My father was extremely happy to see all those gardening articles and he showed it to all his friends, even at our native town Sambalpur. For me, the nostalgia did not fade so easily and in every opportunity, I was recapitulating those memories and was narrating it to my friends and family members.

Chapter 3:

Lizards and Shark Fins in the Far East

Describing, the experience of more than a month's stay in Europe among friends and relatives, continued for about 2 months. Then I remained busy in the daily grind of the Plant and gradually got occupied with other activities. During that period, my daughters were 10 years and 5 years of age. Time passed by and in 1997, our company brought a policy that one can go by flight with their family on Leave Travel Concession (LTC) to the Andamans, irrespective of rank and eligibility. This was a great opportunity for me to go to the Andaman Islands, with family by air, as I was not eligible during those days to avail Leave Travel Concession for flights. Many of the employees, like me, applied for it and it was being given on a first come first serve basis. I was obviously in the queue and was likely to get it in February 1998. But to my bad luck, the scheme got stopped due to a crunch of funds in our company. I had promised my children to take them on flight and hence they were greatly disappointed. I then explored the expenditure for about 5/6 days' visit to Andaman and was trying to organise the funds, as I had promised to my children.

That April after the examinations of the children, we visited my in-law's place at Bhubaneswar. A friend of my sister-in-law, whose name was 'Jishu' visited us. During the conversation, he could know about our programme, which could not materialise, and that I was planning to visit Andaman, from my pocket. He had then just returned from a

Bangkok and Pattaya trip and strongly recommended to go for a 6nights/7days trip to Bangkok and Pattaya. I was wondering if I could afford it. Jishu said the approximate cost and I was surprised to know how affordable it was. It was at that moment only, that, I decided to go ahead. But I had to curtail the duration of the visit to 5 nights/6 days due to a fund crunch.

Then both of us went to the Sita Kunoi Travel agent at Bapuji Nagar, Bhubaneswar. Jishu introduced me to one of their officers named Bishnu. He promised to make the best possible package for me. I came home and revealed the proposal. My children were overjoyed with the proposal. But my wife was a bit apprehensive and had several questions in her mind, primarily about money. I said, not to worry and that I would take care of everything. The first stage was, the period of visit and we decided to go during Durga Puja time, which was October 1998. Except for me, neither my wife nor my children had a passport then. There was a lot of difficulty in making 3 passports and finally, we got all the passports by end of May 1998. I knew that the next hurdle would be to arrange money for such a trip, though I had a little amount of saving. With a lot of courage, I went to Bhubaneswar in the 1st week of June and went straight to Sita Travels and met Mr. Bishnu, again. We had a detailed discussion about the total programme. Finally, I decided to have the programme for 5nights / 6 days to Bangkok and Pattaya. However, Jishu had put in a word to Mr. Bishnu to give me the best possible deal. Along with all passports I paid a little money in advance and came back to Rourkela. I was still short of funds as per the tentative estimate and I was not able to decide, how to arrange the rest of the money. After reaching Rourkela, I thought about it deeply and checked for a Provident Fund loan. As there was a provision of temporary loan, I thought, that to be the best option to avail Provident Fund loan. I applied for a loan from my Provident fund account and got it within a week. I was then totally relaxed and sure of the trip.

I received all my documents with air tickets, vouchers, etc., by the 25th of September and was absolutely ready to take off from Rourkela. In October 1998, we went to Calcutta by train and the next day our flight was scheduled at 2:30 pm by Thai Airways. After all the formalities, we boarded the flight with full excitement. That was the debut visit abroad for my wife and my daughters. For my daughters, it was the debut journey by flight too. It was so thrilling to sit inside the aircraft before going to travel a foreign soil along with family, which can't really be described with justice. Both my daughters put the headphones into their ears and then the plane took off. I will never forget the expression of my daughters and particularly, the younger one, during the take-off of the flight. Her face looked like she had butterflies in her stomach, she was that excited. The inflight service was a new experience for my 2 daughters and they were taking permission from their mother, before ordering anything. It was just a 2 ½ hour flight from Calcutta to Bangkok and hence, around 5 pm (India time) we were asked to change our time in the flight itself while landing. Thailand is an hour and a half ahead of India and when we landed at the Bangkok International Airport, it was around 6 pm. Along with the family, it was a different experience to land in Bangkok, completing the immigration formalities, and walking through the exit. The airport was not as big as Charles de Gaulle Airport, Paris, Schiphol, Amsterdam or Heathrow, London, which I had seen in 1996. But then it was a new experience for my children and wife. The unique experience in the airport was witnessing its cleanliness and the orchids flower all around.

The moment we came out of the exit gate, we found one gentleman standing with a plaque card with my name on it. Then he escorted us to his car. It was a beautiful huge Toyota SUV and was very spacious. Both my daughters preferred to sit in the back row. I and my wife sat in the middle row, behind the driver. The driver delivered all the vouchers and coupons for all the days. Then we proceeded directly to Pattaya, which was about 150km away. We were very comfortable in the taxi and the taxi took us to a petrol pump, where he filled diesel and asked us to take some refreshments if we so desire. All of us went to the departmental store attached to the petrol pump. Though I had the experience of such stores in Europe, it was a new experience for my children. They bought fruits, chips and stuff like that for the road. We then proceeded to the highway and I was having a conversation with the driver about Pattaya and Thailand in general. By some time, both my daughters and my wife slept in the vehicle. I found the driver, to be very interesting and continued talking. It took around 2 ½ hours and an awesome drive and we finally reached the hotel in Pattaya.

The next day, our programme was to go to the Coral Islands in Pattaya. With all excitement, we were waiting in the lobby and a person came around 10 am. We simply showed the coupons to that man and he took us in a vehicle to the seashore, to the meeting point. About 40 tourists gathered at the point and then all of us boarded a small cruise to go to the Coral Islands. The distance between Pattaya and Coral Islands is around 7km in the sea and it took around one hours on the cruise. It was a lovely trip in the sea with tourists from different countries on board. My daughters developed a friendship with many of them during the journey and were very thrilled. I had carried fruits, cold drinks etc. in my bag pack. We started having fruits and cold drinks on board and finally, we reached the island around 12.30 pm. By then we were feeling hungry and had our food in the small huts made for the tourists as restaurants on the seashore.

After food and lying down on the sea beach for some time, we went to the sea for bathing and swimming. Both my daughters were very good swimmers and enjoyed themselves thoroughly. Since I was not a good swimmer, I spent my time in shallow water. Several water sports were available on the sea. We took only a water scooter, which appeared to be very safe. But to our surprise, we could not see proper coral on the route to the islands, nor in the island itself. The local inhabitants, explained that a couple of years ago, the fishermen had put low intensity dynamites to catch fish and, in that process, all the corals died. Subsequently, Thailand Government had stopped fishing in that area to attract tourists, but by then, the corals were already dead and destroyed. However, dead coral which was white in colour was visible, but it was in parts that the actual green coral was visible.

Having spent the whole day there, we started from the island around 4:30 pm and reached Pattaya around 7 pm. We were totally tired and straight went to the hotel. We took a rest and around 9 pm we asked in the reception about some good eating joints nearby. The receptionist guided us to go to a nearby food market. The place was absolutely safe and we walked through the streets and reached there within 10 minutes. We found different food stalls selling all kinds of food including seafood. Most of the people moving around were tourists. A live band and accompanying dance were going on in its full glory. It was something very new for us and was truly a happening place. My children were enjoying the environment. I asked them to stand in one place and enjoy the band. Then I started searching for something to eat. I could choose only 2 stalls where probably we all could eat. I called my family to one stall that I chose. A middle-aged lady was selling seafood including fish fry etc. Jokingly, I asked if she is selling "Jhitpiti", which meant lizard, in our native language. She could not understand and my children were laughing loudly. The lady thought we were ridiculing her and became angry. Then, of course we ate fish fries from her stall. That was one of the most memorable and eventful things that happened that night in Pattaya. Then we went to the 2nd stall that I had chosen. In that stall, different types of burgers were available. We had burgers and then fruit juice and came back to the hotel. We were told that the place that we had gone to, is open throughout the night. But, being with my family including small children, I did not venture to stay longer and came back to the hotel by 10:30 pm.

The next day we were supposed to come to Bangkok by road. The vehicle came around 11 am and we started for Bangkok. The journey from Pattaya to Bangkok was more enjoyable than the journey from Bangkok to Pattaya. It was simply because this was a day time journey where we could witness the beauty of the road while the latter was a night-time journey where we were mostly tired and could not enjoy anything. We reached Bangkok at around 3 pm, as we came quite leisurely and also had lunch on our way. Our booking was in a hotel named 'Hotel Hampton Inn', which was nice and star hotel located almost in the centre of the city. We were given a suite on the 5th floor which was very spacious with a huge room. The whole city was visible from the room and the lighting of the city was just great.

That evening we moved around the streets and discovered different food joints. It was very typical of Bangkok streets that we saw a lot of seafood hawkers, who were selling snails, squids, etc. But we found one Iranian food joint selling 'Severma'. We found it to be the best available food and got the chicken severma packed and bought bananas, which we brought back to our room. I, along with my wife and children relished the food. The next morning, we had the conducted tour in and around Bangkok, which also included an 'Amusement Park'. Our vehicle was supposed to come at 10 am. Before that, we went to the dining place for our breakfast. The place was on the 1st floor and had a beautiful ambience with creepers and orchids-filled glass panes. The spread of the breakfast was awesome with hot breakfast being served. My children were thrilled to see all this and we all had a heavy breakfast. Then we proceeded for the day's tour. They took us to some beautiful Buddhist temples, gardens, palaces, etc. Finally, in the second half, they took us to the Amusement Park as decided. The entry ticket was pre-booked. It was such a fantastic place, full of different rides and games like 'Roller coaster', 'Columbus' and many others. First, we went around the place and saw all rides. Then we chose to sit on the 'Columbus'. It was a rocking ride and the oscillation was gradually being increased with a full blast of music. It was very exciting and thrilling and we all were laughing loudly and enjoying the ride. Suddenly, my wife Rachita started feeling giddy and having a nautical effect. I shouted to the ride operator to stop the game. Gradually, the oscillation was reduced, but by then she had thrown up all over her dress and the dupatta. We then sat beneath a tree and my wife washed her face and drank some water. After half an hour, she felt comfortable and again we went around for different rides. Finally, we went to a place having 'Dashing car' rides or bumper cars. There was no risk, but Rachita did not venture and I along with both my daughters sat on the ride and had loads of fun.

That was the last tourist attraction for the day and we spent the entire second half in that amusement park and came back to the hotel by 6 pm. We took rest and did not go anywhere for dinner. We ordered some food in our hotel and ate in the room. The next day, we went to the biggest market complex called 'International Trade Centre'. It was nothing but a huge shopping mall with several international brands and some offices. But we had never seen such a market complex in India and it was something new for my family. We did some shopping and then went to the local market place.

That market was crowded and had all types of articles that we could buy. We were told that 'Thai silk' is very famous and we could see several garments including neckties, etc., made out of Thai silk. We bought few shirts for gifts and I bought two neckties for myself. We bought several things from there and came back to the hotel at around 5 pm. We spent the whole day visiting marketplaces and shopping. We took rest and decided to go to a continental joint for dinner to have Thai delicacies. Again, we walked through the streets and searched for a good restaurant. We went inside a place and 4 of us sat at the table. The typical smell of seafood lingered there which was literally a stink for us. Although we wanted to go away from there, we sat for a while to see the menu to find out the availability of food items. I had read about 'shark fin soup' and saw it on the menu. After seeing the menu and the astronomical price, we simply said, "Thank you", and went away. I thought of going to another sea food joint, but my children were not interested. In that area, we were getting the smell of seafood and particularly lemongrass. That smell was something very typical of Bangkok. Finally, only because of typical smell and my children's choice, we found the 'Severma' and a 'Kewab' joint to be the safest and the best place to eat. This time we did not take away and had it there itself.

The next day was our flight back to Calcutta, India. It was overall an amazing experience and we got ready to come to the airport after having our breakfast. We then started for the airport as our flight was at 2:30 pm. The driver got delayed and we were anxiously waiting in the hotel lobby. Finally, we reached the airport around 1 pm and there was not much time in hand. We could not buy any item including chocolate, etc., from the duty-free shops. Our names were being announced to board the flight and we literally ran to board the flight. Finally, we were the last 4 passengers to board the flight. But to our surprise, the flight did not take off even after the scheduled departure and we all were sitting in the aircraft. Finally, it was announced at 3 pm that there was a technical snag and the flight would take off at 4 pm. Finally, it took off at 4:30 pm and it was a great relief for us. Around 5 pm (IST) we landed in Calcutta. One of my cousins, Sushri, was living in Gariahaat area of Calcutta. From the airport, we straight went to her house and spent the night with them. The next morning, we came back to Rourkela by Ispat Express. Even today, both my daughters recapitulate the "Jhitpiti" (Lizard) episode of Pattaya, and we all laugh loudly with those sweet memories.

Chapter 4:

Science, Arts, or Commerce?

I always told both my daughters that they could go for a pleasure trip to see foreign lands with their parents at a very young age. In fact, the travel experience to Bangkok and Pattaya was something very special for them and even today, they cherish the sweet memories of their experience. With the kind of salary that I was getting, it was a difficult task for me to travel to foreign soil with family and my children gradually realised that. I said, if they would study well and earn decent money, they can travel the whole world and I had simply given them exposure to a foreign land That word of mine was truly impregnated in their mind.

In 1998, when we went to Thailand, my elder and younger daughters were of 12 years and 7 years of age respectively. That was the time when they should concentrate on their studies and Rachita and I decided to focus on their studies. We stopped even our domestic travel for a couple of years. In 1999, my elder daughter said, she would pursue Arts after 10th grade (ICSE) and that she is not interested in Mathematics at all. We as parents were a bit surprised, but allowed her to study her subjects of interest, at the same time, persuaded her to study Mathematics, which was mandatory up to class 10. She was a very good story and poem writer, as well as a great debater. She was a child prodigy in that field and even one of her poems was published in a reputed poetry website named "Poetry.com" based in the USA. She never really took any interest in Mathematics. She appeared in the

ICSE examination in 2001. Though she did not get very high score, but scored more than 80%.

Then, she was bent upon studying arts. None of the good schools in Rourkela, including my daughter's school 'Carmel Convent', offered arts at the higher secondary level, i.e., +2. It was only available in our company-run Rourkela Steel Plant school named "Ispat Vaidya Mandir", which did not have ICSE or CBSE course but the 'Odisha State Board' course that is "Council of Higher Secondary Education" CHSE. Rachita was coaxing Anisha to study science, so that later, she could have the option of switching over to whichever stream she wanted to, including arts. But I believed that she should pursue whatever she wants. There was a lot of disturbance in our house regarding this subject. Finally, we went to a professional counsellor to assess her orientation and acumen. That counsellor took 3 sessions, 2 for her individually and the 3rd one was with us and that was the final sitting with the counsellor. He showed us a matrix table and concluded that our daughter's orientation was towards "Arts". Rachita finally got convinced that, our daughter should join Arts.

At that time, she did not have any option but to pursue her studies in that school named 'Ispat Vidya Mandir'. Initially, she was a bit upset that she could not study in a good school. Many of our friends and relatives ridiculed her, that probably she was not a good student and did not get a seat anywhere. Rourkela being a steel city, the orientation of our relatives and people around us, was towards either Medical or Engineering. They could not comprehend that some child would opt to pursue Arts.

But "Man proposes" and "God disposes". She continued +2 at our company-run school "Ispat Vidya Mandir'. She started taking interest in her subjects and participated in several extracurricular activities as well, like, poem writing, elocution, and debate, etc., in addition to her studies. In the 1st quarterly examination, she stood 1st and was extremely happy. We encouraged her and, in her school, all the teachers started liking her. In fact, she was also inspired by one of her seniors, who also studied Arts in the same school and was ranked in the top 20 in the state. In the first-year examination also Anisha stood first not only in academics but also in debate and poem in the inter-school competition. During the annual day function, when she received several prizes in addition to academics, her English teacher, who was speaking on the podium, named her "Versatile genius". That gave my daughter Anisha more encouragement and to us also.

During that period, the Board of Secondary Education, Odisha was conducting the "Chair Man's Cup" Debate Competition among all the +2 colleges in Odisha. She always had the desire not only to become the topper of the school but also wanted to come in the top 20 in Odisha. At the same time, she also wanted to receive the "Chairman's Cup" in the Debate competition. Because, those achievements would fetch her an honour of having the name written in the incumbency chart of the school, in their principal's room.

That was her dream, and she participated in the debate and for that, I had to accompany her to the legendary 'Ravenshaw College' in Cuttack. More than 100 students from different +2 colleges all over Odisha, came for the competition. We were a bit apprehensive and kept our fingers crossed as the competition was very tough. The authorities gave only half an hour for preparation after the topic was declared. Finally, it started and continued for the whole day. We were anxiously waiting for the result, which was declared in the evening. She stood first in that competition and both of us were in the seventh heaven. It was such an unforgettable moment which can't be described in words.

With a huge 'Chairman's Cup', we returned home with glory. Everyone, the family, friends, were all praising my daughter for her achievement. It was a great achievement for her school as well. The next year i.e., in 2003, the +2 final board examination was scheduled to take place. After she received her 'Chairman's Cup' in debate, we also encouraged her to get a rank in the top 20 in the state. Finally, her +2 final result came and she stood 16th in the state and 1st in our Sundargarh district. Her name with photograph was flashed in all local newspapers and hundreds of phone calls came flowing. We all were extremely happy that she made us proud by pursuing Arts and prayed that she should further excel in her life.

She then chose to pursue English Honours and wanted to join "Loyola College", Chennai or "Christ College", Bangalore. But, by the time her result came out, all the admissions were over in those colleges. She did not have any option left and joined "Rama Devi College", Bhubaneswar. In the 1st year, she again stood first. Even, during her college days, she participated in several competitions in elocution and debate etc. and brought lot of laurels for herself and for her institute too. In her graduation, she stood 1st, first class with distinction and was appreciated by one and all. Her focus was then to get into some top Social Sciences colleges in India. Her topmost priority was 'Tata Institute of Social Sciences'(TISS), Mumbai and 'Delhi School of Social Work' for Social Sciences and 'Jamia Millia Islamia', Delhi, for Journalism and Developmental Communication. She applied in only these three places. We were very much worried that she did not apply to any other college. I travelled with her for the Jamia Entrance Examination in Delhi. She, in fact, got a call from the Delhi School of Social Work for admission, which was only on the basis of marks. Again, we went to Mumbai for the TISS examination. There were only 80 seats in TISS and the selection procedure was very tough and lengthy.

One of my co-brothers-in-law was in a senior position in IDBI bank and could manage to get us rooms in a NABARD guest house at Ghat Koper,Mumbai, at a very nominal cost. TISS is situated in Deonar near

Chembur and was relatively nearer to the Guesthouse in Mumbai standards. We stayed in the guest house and the next day went to the TISS campus to get the admit card for the written examination. The next day, she appeared for the written examination, the duration of which was for 3 hours. After the exam, we came back with a lot of speculation. The result was out the next day and she cleared the written exam. The next step was the group discussion on the next day. We were travelling on a local train, and a phone call came that she has cleared even the group discussion round. Both of us were relieved and were waiting for the final interview date. The day the group discussion result was declared was a Friday. The final interview was scheduled for 2 days. One on the Saturday and the other one was on Monday. Incidentally, my daughter's interview was on Monday. So, we had no other option but to wait until Monday.

On Monday, we both prayed to God and went to the campus for the interview. I waited for her interview to be over and she came out, with a gloomy face. I tried to encourage her and we hired an auto-rickshaw and went to a restaurant. We ordered seafood of her choice. On the way, we were only discussing the finale and praying to God. After having lunch, we came back to the guest house and took a rest. At around 7 pm we got a phone call that she has been finally selected in TISS. We hugged each other and cried and said, "God finally gave us the best gift ever possible". We cherished this beautiful moment of our lives and shared the information with our family. Everybody was extremely happy in our family to get the news.

The next morning, Rachita called and said, she has also got into the 'Developmental Communication' course at Jamia Milia Islamia. But, then the first choice was TISS for my daughter. In that process, we stayed for a week at the guest house in Mumbai. That was a unique experience and the longest stay outside Rourkela for any examination. My daughter and I were laughing a lot, the whole experience of a mixed feeling of stress, anxiety, and at the same time happiness and we named the whole event "An Odyssey to TISS". She then joined the institute and was very happy. She had some great experiences in that institute of international repute and spent 2 glorious years there.

My younger daughter, Anooja, right from her childhood was oriented towards law. My father had 2 paternal uncles as lawyers and he always wanted my younger daughter to become a lawyer. The younger one was very witty and for that reason, my father had once said "She would definitely become a lawyer" when she was studying in the 5th grade. She grew up and like her sister, did not want to pursue science after her 10th grade in ICSE. We fulfilled all her desires and when she was in class IX, my wife joined as a teacher in St. Paul's school, adjacent to Anooja's school. My wife Rachita had a long desire to become a teacher. We consciously had decided that focusing on children's studies would be preferred than doing teacher ship. Hence, when our elder daughter Anisha was already studying in +3 at Rama Devi College, Bhubaneswar and the younger one was in class IX and was quite confident of taking care of herself, Rachita decided to take up the job of a teacher in 2005. In fact, both the daughters were able to handle themselves, as we had made them quite independent. Rachita continued her teacher ship and at the same time keeping a watch on the younger daughter. In 2006 Anooja appeared the tenth-grade board exams, ICSE. She did quite well and got 92% marks. She was very focused and wanted to pursue law and like her sister did not want to study Science, though she was quite good at Mathematics too. She wanted to pursue Commerce but the school that she was studying in, did not offer Commerce at that time. She then joined another school nearby named 'St. Joseph School' where Commerce was there in the +2 level.

The subject and school suited her and she was very studious in her studies. Simultaneously, she took admission in online coaching for the law entrance examination, as at that point of time, there was no classroom coaching for law entrance at Rourkela. One way, it was better for her, that she was not required to go out for tuition or coaching, like science students.

Chapter 5:

Twisted Breads and Steep Mountains

Life continued, but at the back of my mind, I had an overwhelming desire to see the USA. I would often hear about the USA from my maternal uncle. He was my mother's elder brother, an alumnus of Indian Institute of Science, Bangalore. He was in a senior position at Rourkela Steel Plant and IISCO Steel Plant, Steel Authority of India Limited (SAIL). He had visited the USA, both in his official capacity and also for pleasure trip. Even my younger maternal uncle, Nirmal, who had gone to the USA for his Masters, after graduating in engineering from IIT, Kharagpur in 1963 and stayed back in USA. He preferred to continue his life in USA and even got married there. Since then, I was inspired and the dream of going to USA had started. Eventually, my younger co-brother-in-law, who is a Computer Science guy, also went to the USA permanently, with his family in December, 1996. The same year that I had visited Europe first time for my training. He was the one who had received me in Delhi after landing in India, in August 1996.

I was always fascinated about both my maternal uncles, that both of them were so acquainted with the USA. Finally, when my younger co-brother-in-law Manoj went to USA in 1996, and was always describing about the great quality of life there, the urge to go to USA got further enhanced. Nevertheless, right from my child hood, I never wanted to settle and live in any foreign soil. I always wanted to go to places as a tourist and enjoy the life out there. I first wrote to Manoj in 2006, that both my daughters are now old enough, and that I & Rachita would be able to visit them, the next year in 2007. He, at first instance did not take me seriously, as normally people would not visit USA on a pleasure trip, during those days. The next Saturday he called me, and we had a long talk and he could read my mind. Now he was sure that I was determined to visit him soon. Then the paper work started for the USA visa. In the meantime, I discussed with Rachita and said that, I had not visited Switzerland during my debut visit to Europe in 1996, during the training at Germany and would like to visit Switzerland too, enroute USA. She also agreed and was very happy. Thereafter, I started my preparation.

I talked to one of my cousin sisters, Tikli, who lives in Zurich, and made a plan for 3 days stay at Switzerland. Since, I had decided to go to Switzerland, I booked my air ticket by Swiss air. For the Swiss visa, I approached M/s Thomas Cook at Kolkata and they said, it would be very easy to obtain Swiss visa, provided we get the USA visa. It was in October 2006, that we went to Kolkata for our visa with all the required documents. I had not taken any help from any Travel agent for the USA visa. Rachita and I stood in a long queue and thought that probably it would be evening by the time the interview is over. But it was very systematic and within 2 hours, everything was completed. When we went inside, the security was very strict, and finally we were interviewed by a lady. She asked several questions and even asked, why I have booked my air ticket, beforehand, without even obtaining the USA visa. After listening from the lady, it was a very big suspense for us, whether we would be granted visa or not. The Passport duly stamped with the visa, was supposed to have been obtained from another office, the next day, as per procedure. Next day we went another office and when, we opened the packet, we were surprised to get 10 years' visa for USA. That was a great moment for us. Immediately, we went to Thomas Cook's office to have our discussion on the Switzerland visa and trip. One young girl in M/s Thomas Cook office helped us a lot and asked us to book a hotel to facilitate Switzerland visa. She showed us different options and finally we gave priority to the location. The hotel that we booked was 'X-Tra', which was a very decent hotel and centrally located.

Finally, we organised everything that was required for the tour, through M/s Thomas Cook. We made a meticulous plan for our trip. Our flight was scheduled from Mumbai by Swiss Air. It was June end 2007, that we were supposed to go to Switzerland and by then all the papers should have been in hand. During those days, the passport was being sent to Delhi office for visa stamping for Switzerland visa as it was not covered under Schengen countries. We had booked our train ticket to Mumbai from Rourkela, because of heavy luggage and it was much easier to go to Mumbai directly from Rourkela, by train, where we live.

But, to our bad luck, the visa and other vouchers, did not reach by courier at Rourkela on time, though I had planned everything well in advance. There were only 3 days left for our flight from Mumbai to Switzerland and we had not yet received the Swiss visa stamped passport. Though, I was constantly following up with M/s Thomas Cook, I could not get the visa on time. It was a great shock and stress for us at the last moment. Finally, I got a call from the same young lady that, our Passport stamped with visa was lying in the courier office and it was delivered to Thomas Cook on that very day only. Since only 3 days were left, there was no option left and I had to cancel my train ticket and asked Thomas cook to book air ticket from Kolkata to Mumbai for me and my wife. Accordingly, we proceeded to Kolkata by train the same night and the next day we collected all papers, tickets and the visa and were extremely relieved. We also exchanged US dollars for our travel and at that time 1 USD amounted to around Rupees 45.00 only.

We flew on the same night to Mumbai, as our flight to Zurich from Mumbai was at 1.30 am, the next day. We reached Mumbai and stayed with one of my brothers-in-law, the same gentleman who had arranged the NABARD guest house for us during the TISS examination of my daughter Anisha. Next morning, our elder daughter Anisha, who was studying in TISS, visited us and we had lunch together. The same night, we flew to Zurich. I and my wife were relaxed and had a nice flight of about 8 hours. At around 9 am Swiss time, we reached at Zurich. It was a beautiful airport and we were so excited to see my cousin sister Tikli and her husband at the airport. They had come to receive us at Zurich, a foreign land, which was truly very thrilling for us. They dropped us at our hotel 'X-Tra' and my brother-in-law, went to his office directly from the hotel after dropping us. My cousin sister Tikli stayed back with us. After we got freshened up and took a bit rest, Tikli took us to several locations, as we had much time in hand. She took us to a market place nearby, where a lot of restaurants were located in one place. She said that the 'Swiss twisted bread' is very famous in Switzerland, which is nothing but a bread type eatable and called "Croissant". Several varieties of 'Twisted bread' were available and we had it with different combinations and then finally we had coffee. While sitting out there, the three of us made a detailed plan for the next 3 days and Tikli helped us in planning it in the best way.

After discussion in the restaurant during breakfast, Tikli took us to the Zurich Lake. The lake is one of the major landmarks and it was very famous. Since, Tikli had some other jobs, she preferred to leave, after explaining everything nicely to us. After she left, we took a one-hour ride in a cruise. We had walked a long distance prior to boarding the cruise and I was tired. It was a pleasant ride and the weather was also fantastic. After, the ride we, bought all the tickets for the next day and then we went to a beautiful kiosk near the Zurich Lake and had some food and relaxed. By then it was 4 pm and we came back to the hotel and took rest. Tikli and her husband again came to the hotel around 8 pm with lots of food for us. It was such a good experience to have an impromptu food to gather in our hotel. They told us all the details and literally wrote everything about our travel, on a piece of paper for our convenience.

Next morning, after having breakfast, Rachita and I were on our own and first went to the Zurich main railway station. The station was looking like a palace and was absolutely clean. We boarded the train and went to Lucerne, which took about 40 minutes from Zurich. It was a beautiful old and famous city, where they have preserved the medieval architecture with the river "Ruess" at the centre of the city. We walked through the streets and market places. We crossed a wooden heritage bridge named "Chapel Bridge" and took lot of photographs in that compact city. The bridge even had many paintings inside, which seemed very unique to us. It is the world's oldest surviving truss bridge. The place was very typical and had something different to see. A lot of flower vendors were selling different varieties of flowers in the streets.

 After spending some time at Lucerne, we boarded a train from Lucerne to Interlaken which is called 'Golden pass' route in Switzerland. This route was one of the most beautiful and scenic route. The train journey was about 2 hours and the panoramic view through the large windows, was just great. Interlaken is one of the most popular tourist destinations in Switzerland. We moved through crystal clear mountain lakes like Sarnersee lake, Lungernsee lake and Brienz lake, that gather the water from various rivers and water falls. In the mountain area, while going in the steep zone, the train changes to cog wheel drive train technology, in order to conquer the gradient. The Luzern Interlaken express was a part of the scenic Golden Pass line leading to Interlaken. The beautiful ice-covered mountain clip and the green landscape during the journey was just superb. Rachita and I were enjoying a lot and discussing about the Hindi movies' shooting at

Switzerland. It was a like a movie that we were seeing in the train journey and were in a hallucination stage, as if we were in a different world. We reached Interlaken at around 3 pm and walked from the station to the main small town. We walked through the streets and a nearby village and thoroughly enjoyed the place. The whole place was surrounded by mountains and was much cooler than Zurich and Lucerne. We went to a small and beautiful coffee shop and had pastry and coffee there. The taste was great and the amazing ambience added flavour to it.

We came out from the coffee shop and walked through different places and saw a unique thing. In 2 mini trucks a group of people came with reasonably big trees. They brought several machines and dug the earth and planted those trees. I was very inquisitive and asked one man, as to what they were doing. He replied, those trees they grow in a nursery and plant it by the side of the road for beautification and afforestation as well. We were amazed to listen this from him. In Interlaken we could also enjoy the Swiss heritage with majestic views of the Alps. That day we were extremely satisfied to see such beauty of the place. By that time, it was around 6 pm and we boarded our train for the return journey. We reached the hotel around 8 pm and took rest after a hectic yet great day.

The next morning, it was a Saturday and we were invited by Tikli for lunch. We went to their place as they had properly guided us to the location of their house. We had a homely lunch and played with their 2 beautiful children, a son of 8 years and a daughter of 5 years of age. We had a great time at their place and then they wanted to give us a surprise. Around 2:30 pm after lunch, they took out their car and asked us to accompany them. On the way, they said we were proceeding to the 'Rhine Fall'. It took about 45 minutes and reached the spot around 3:30 pm. It was such a huge and beautiful waterfall at the border of Switzerland. It was a breath-taking and stupendous beauty and the largest plain water fall in Europe. The falls were located on the High Rhine at Neuhausen town. There was a huge observation platform from where we got a special opportunity to get closer to the impressive scenic beauty and took a lot of photographs. Then we came back from there and they dropped us at our hotel at around 6:30 pm. To our surprise, again they gave us 2 beautiful mementos of Switzerland, one being a famous 'Cowbell' and the other one was a 'Ceramic souvenir round plate'. We were touched to see all those things and with the overall hospitality shown by them. The overall trip of Switzerland was just great because of their help and support.

Chapter 6:

Red Wine, Pink Bands, and Indians in America

After having a fantastic visit of Switzerland in Europe, our next destination was USA. The same day our flight was scheduled to go to the USA at 10:30 pm. Hence, hurriedly we got ready and rushed to Zurich airport by 7 pm. We boarded our flight from Zurich by American airlines operated by Swiss air. The flight duration was around 8 hours 30 minutes. We reached New York JFK airport around 3 pm (New York time). Before we proceeded to New York, my maternal uncle Nirmal, had said, if we can have a ticket to Newark instead of New York, it would be nearer for him to receive us. However, we had our ticket booked from Zurich to JFK airport New York, much before.

Finally, we landed in JFK airport and landing in the USA was altogether a different experience, as that was one of my dream destinations. We passed through the immigration and when we went to collect our baggage from the belt, we found that our bags were half open and were in shambles. It was too disappointing for us. But when we checked the bags, all articles were intact and that was the biggest relief for us. My maternal uncle Nirmal was waiting outside anxiously and he was guiding us through his mobile phone all the while to the place he was standing. JFK was too busy and huge an airport, but not very clean, as compared to the airports in Europe.

Finally, we could see my uncle and were so excited that we left our luggage behind and hugged him. Then we went to the car parking area and he drove down to his house at Mendham, New Jersey. We discussed our experiences about the total journey and he was also very thrilled listening to us. At the age of 68, he was very fit and drove for about 2 hours to reach his house. The roads were very wide and it was a great experience. On the way, we also saw an abandoned old steel plant, which fascinated me, I being from a steel plant in India. We reached around 6 pm at his house. It was a huge bungalow-type house and the passage to get into the house was through the garage. The best part was that, from his car itself he opened the shutter of his garage, with a remote control. I had never seen such a device and for me and Rachita, it was amazing to have such an experience. We went inside his house and our aunty gave us a warm welcome. Around 7.30 pm, my uncle asked me, if I would like to have some wine. Though I was very liberated, still I could not answer spontaneously and just smiled. He could read my mind and again asked, whether I would have red wine or white wine. I said I would have red wine. I enjoyed the wine with my uncle and then we had our dinner.

After dinner, he gave us a house tour and also showed us the basement. I found a centralised air-conditioning system and some sundry items. But the most surprising part was to see more than 200 bottles of different varieties of wine. I was very happy of being assured of having different types of wines during our stay. Every evening we had wine before dinner and were enjoying it like anything. I could realize that there can be so many varieties of wine that tasted different.

As we stayed with my uncle for several days, he had made a meticulous planning for all the days, which was a great surprise for us. The very next when I got up in the morning, it sunk to my mind that the previous night, I slept in the land of the USA, which was the greatest dream of my life. I was dancing with joy and was enjoying the pure air in his huge garden. I then went to the backyard of my uncle's house and saw that it was a forest. Inside the lush green forest, I was surprised to see even a deer. It was indeed an amazing sight in the morning.

We had our breakfast and that day uncle took us to a nearby market place and we did some random shopping. After that, we had lunch in an Indian restaurant. The buffet lunch in that Indian restaurant was just awesome. I discovered something typical in that restaurant, that once you take one plate and take food on the plate from the spread, after having food, if you want a second serving, then you have to take another fresh plate. I asked my uncle about that culture, which was slightly different than India. My uncle replied that the culture is prevalent all over the USA. After finishing a sumptuous lunch, we came back home at around 5 pm. That evening we spent our time at home and made a conscious plan to talk to different friends and relatives.

The next morning after breakfast, my uncle asked us to get ready and said, we would go to visit a university. I could not comprehend, why he was taking us to a university campus. I could not resist and asked him, why were we going to a university? On the way, he replied, we would be going to the University of Princeton. I was just amazed, as I knew it is one of the top universities and many US Presidents studied there, including John F. Kennedy. I was very excited about the visit and it took us about an hour's drive and we reached there at around noon. The ambience of the university was just great with full of trees and there was a big landmark carved stone named 'Oval with points', where we took photographs. That is one of the outdoor sculptures of the Princeton University. There were several beautiful sculptures which were named 'John B. Putnam, Jr. Memorial Collection of Sculptures'.

Then we started walking through the University campus and enjoyed ourselves a lot. To see the students and the professors moving and taking classes was wonderful. After walking through the campus, we felt thirsty and wanted to drink water and my uncle asked us to drink from a small machine. I did not even know how to operate that water machine. My uncle explained that one has to press a button just beneath the basin portion and water will flow from a small bent pipe at the top. One has to put his or her mouth directly into the water trajectory coming out from the bent tube and drink water. There was no provision of glass to drink water. We used that drinking water machine in the year 2007 and nowadays we can find those in the Indian airports for drinking water. That was something unique that I saw for the first time inside the university campus. Then we came back from the university and had our lunch on the way. We reached home at about 5 pm after a beautiful day.

The next day, we simply chilled and spent the whole day at home and my aunty was busy making several dishes since morning. We all including our uncle helped her in cooking. In fact, my uncle had invited one of his old friends and his wife for dinner, in honour of our arrival at his house in the USA. On that day, the dish washer did not work and my aunty struggled a lot and was worried that, the same evening, had invited guest to their house. She just showed me the machine and I could fix it within 10 minutes. She was extremely relieved and thrilled. On a lighter note, she started ridiculing my uncle, that he could not have fixed it. After the repair episode, in the meantime, we sat in his garden and spent the sunny day. Since it was the month of June, the garden was in full bloom and was very beautiful.

The same evening, my uncle's guests arrived exactly at 6:30 pm. I was surprised to see my watch, as it was too early and at the same time, because of their punctuality. My uncle introduced me and Rachita to the couple. The gentleman was of Indian origin and his wife was American. They were a lovely and very warm couple. That evening, all 6 of us sat in the drawing-room, which was the first time for us, sitting in the drawing-room, like all the other times, we were sitting in the dining space or the garden. That evening, we started with white wine and some good snacks. The sparkling white wine had a very nice taste. After having wine, we also had a little of Glen Fiddich (18 years) Single Malt whisky. That evening, it was very interesting to listen to the experiences of my uncle and his friend, how they came to the USA in the early sixties and how they had struggled in their initial phase when very few Indians immigrated to the USA. Both of them rose to great heights in their respective fields, after doing their Masters in the USA. Rachita and I were listening to their experiences very carefully and were thrilled. It was an amazing experience to listen to their real-life stories. My aunty and the other lady were sometimes also supplementing the true story and were becoming emotional. We were so much engrossed in talking that we forgot the time. My aunty reminded us to have dinner and by that time, it was already 10.30 pm. Then we started having dinner and my uncle informed us at the dining table about the next day's programme of going to New York.

We then finished our dinner and had our dessert. It was around midnight by the time my uncle's friend and his wife left for their home and we could retire to our beds. My uncle said, "Tomorrow we have to get ready by 9 am". I was taken aback, as after being late and with a heavy dinner, it would be very difficult to get up early and get ready by 9 am. But then, the excitement of visiting a new place like 'New York' was in the back of our mind and we got up quite early at around 6 am. I was feeling fresh in the morning after a good night's sleep and the thought of going to 'New York' made us more energetic. After breakfast, all 4 of us started for New York around 9 am. The drive was extremely pleasant and we reached New York at around 10.30 am. My uncle had booked some tickets for us and after he collected those from a travel agent in the Manhattan area, he took us to the harbour area. That area was a great place and he handed us 2 tickets for me and Rachita and said "Enjoy the cruise ride". Then, both my uncle and aunt went to a theatre and asked us to meet at a particular point after our trip was over.

In the harbour area, a lot of tourists were there and were enjoying in their ways. We asked about the departure of our cruise and found that it was of a duration of 2 hours and would start after half an hour. Since we had half an hour in hand, we went to explore different eating and drinking joints and we took some snacks. We then boarded the cruise and it started moving with joy with an audio system narrating the whole journey. The cruise started proceeding towards 'Statue of Liberty' and it was truly very enjoyable. We reached near the iconic 'Statue of Liberty' and saw the world-famous gigantic statue. It was an amazing sight and we took several photographs. The cruise stopped near the statue for about 10 minutes and the history was being narrated. The cruise then started returning from that spot and the return journey was equally enjoyable. I discovered the bar on the cruise on our return journey and had a can of beer. Around 2:30 pm we reached the coast and went to the spot that my uncle had shown. We boarded the car and four of us went for lunch, though we were not hungry. We had a little food and then my uncle said, "Let us go to the Empire State Building". We thought he would simply drive through. But he parked the car and all 4 of us went inside and to the topmost floor of the Empire State Building. We enjoyed the view of the whole of New York City including the harbour and the Statue of Liberty from the top of the 'Empire State Building'. We took a lot of photographs from the top and also at the boom base of the building. There was a miniature 'Empire state building' at the entrance in the base where also we took a lot of photographs. Around 5 pm we started our return journey. On our way back, my uncle showed us the twin towers, which were destroyed during the 9/11 episode and it was under construction. We then proceeded home, after a memorable trip to New York. We were very tired that day and after having a little food, we went to sleep quite early.

At around 6 pm, when we were on our way home to my uncle's place, my co-brother-in-law Manoj called my uncle on his mobile. My uncle passed on the phone to me. Manoj, was living near Washington DC. He gave me a surprise and said he would come the next day to take us to their house at Gettysburg near Washington DC. As per the original programme, he was supposed to come after 2 days, but he preponed his programme. My uncle had made different programmes for us in the next 2 days. But he did not want to disappoint Manoj and agreed to the proposal. The reason that he wanted to take us to Gettysburg was that my sister-in-law had booked tickets for a nice concert. Rachita called her sister and asked, why she had suddenly changed the programme and preponed the visit. With full excitement, she replied, as we are music lovers, which she knew, she has booked tickets for a concert of A R Rahman. Rachita & I felt like jumping to the sky. My uncle and aunt were amused to see our childlike behaviour to know about the A R Rahman's show. That night being the last night of our stay at my uncle's house, after dinner we talked about different sweet memories late into the night.

The next day, early morning, Manoj started from his house at Gettysburg with his new car, which he had bought recently. It was a limited edition of SUV of Toyota. He too was very excited to drive about 200 miles by his new car to receive us at my uncle's house. He had started at around 7.30 am and reached Mendham at my uncle's house at around 10 am. After our breakfast and packing our luggage, we were ready to receive him. We all had some apprehension, as to whether he would be able to locate the house easily and my uncle was in constant touch with him through the mobile phone. Finally, he reached and when we asked him if he faced any difficulty in locating the house, he simply laughed and said, "My voice-activated GPS in the car brought me here very easily". For me, it was very surprising to see the voice-activated GPS in his car, during those days. Manoj freshened up after about 3 hours of driving and again we started towards Gettysburg at around noon.

When we reached the highway, it was worth seeing as both sides were jungle with lush green trees and a black smooth road in between. In most of the places between the roadside and the jungle, there were barricades to prevent animals from coming onto the road, particularly deer. We could see a lot of deer in the extremely beautiful, lush green jungle. In the middle of the highway, we even saw one dead deer, which probably had somehow come to the highway and had died in an accident after being hit by any vehicle. Nevertheless, the drive was very nice and we reached Manoj's place around 3:30 pm. When we reached their home, it was worth seeing both the sisters hugging each other and crying, not able to comprehend seeing each other in the USA. It was just a great nostalgic feeling to see the warm welcome by my sister-in-law, Ishita, and the whole family.

The best part was, that on the same evening at 7 pm, the A R Rahman concert was scheduled and we were supposed to reach the venue half an hour before the programme. The venue was called 'Patriot Centre' in Virginia and the commuting distance was around 45 minutes from Manoj & Ishita's place. Hence, we got ready and started for the show, around 5:30 pm. We reached there and I found that it's a very huge hall. We went inside and saw that several varieties of Indian snacks like Samosa, Kachori, etc., were available along with other non-alcoholic and alcoholic beverages. We could take those articles inside the hall also. I wanted to have a beer and Manoj took several of snacks. When I asked for a beer, the salesman looked at my face and gave it and put a pink band on my hand. That was very funny for me and when I asked, it was clarified that one should be above the age of 18 years, which of course I was, and the second reason was to differentiate the drinkers and non-drinkers. We went inside the hall and the show started exactly at 7 pm and it was a 2-hours show. It would have been impossible for me to see such a programme and have such an experience in India, as we live in a small town named Rourkela, in the western part of Odisha in India. Rachita and I being music lovers, vividly remember the names of the artist and the total programme, which is deeply engraved in our mind. When A R Rahman, appeared on the stage, it was a lifetime experience and it was so humbling. The programme was a memorable one with great legendary artists. To name those who were present were, Sukhvinder Singh, S P Balasubramaniam, Hariharan, Chitra, and the great drummer Sivamani. The enchanting melodious voice of the singers including A R Rahman and magical beats of the drum by Sivamani made everybody spellbound. We returned home after such a mega show and were talking about it for the next 2 days. In fact, that particular day was so interesting and hectic that we could not even take out all our luggage. The next day, we opened the articles, one by one to show them, whatever gift and food articles that we had taken from India for them. I could see the excitement in the faces of Ishita and the cute children.

The house of Manoj and Ishita, that we went to was newly bought by them. It was a beautiful double-storeyed house in a beautiful location. Incidentally, when we went to their house, they had just completed living for only 1 week in the new house. Hence, they performed the 'Griha Prabesh Puja' after our arrival. The 'Hindu Priest' came in a big Toyota car, wearing saffron clothes, and performed the puja. It was very interesting and surprising too, for us in the USA.

 The location of Manoj's place was great, situated in a prime location. As, on the first day of our arrival, we were busy with the musical programme, we relaxed the next day. Manoj went to his office and we simply chilled and discussed a tentative programme during our stay in the USA. We were so surprised to listen from Ishita that our whole stay has been micro planned by them. That day, Ishita after lunch took us to a nearby marketplace called RIO. It was an amazing place having a community museum, water park, shopping complex, restaurants, and pubs. We spent about 3 hours in that place and thoroughly enjoyed it. We then came home at around 6 pm. Manoj came from his office at around 7 pm and then we had a detailed discussion about what our programme would be during the stay. The discussion part over a glass of wine was more interesting than, probably the actual visits to different places. As they had 5 working days and Saturday being a holiday, our 1st Saturday's programme was 'Luray Caverns' which is a huge cave in Luray in the state of Virginia.

Post lunch, we started for the Luray Caverns in their new SUV. That was the first long journey of about 2 hours after the journey for the A R Rahman concert, on the very first day of our arrival. We started at around 2 pm from their house and reached the Luray Caverns at around 4 pm. As usual, the journey was great and the place is a tourist spot, was bit crowded. When we went inside the cave, it was just mind-blowing with different coloured rocks. The cave had columns, mudflows, stalactites, stalagmites, flowstones, and also mirrored pools. This cavern was discovered in 1887 and is one of the largest caves in the USA. It was a different experience to walk inside such a cave for more than an hour and seeing all the combinations of colours with different shapes and sizes of rocks. After having spent a memorable day, we came back home at around 8 pm.

The next day being a Sunday, our visit was a beach resort named 'Rehoboth'. We had a heavy breakfast a bit late in the morning (a brunch) and started in the SUV at around 12:30 in the afternoon. The climate was suitable for a visit to the beach. However, the commuting time was around 3 hours. On that day, Ishita was driving the car, and obviously, the GPS was on. When we reached near the beach, she went through a road which was a bit narrow as compared to other roads in that area and we reached a place, where a lot of temporary huts and small houses were there and we could not reach the beach. Manoj had a doubt and asked his wife to reboot the GPS and come back from the locality. It was discovered that the locality was meant for senior citizens and all were relaxing in those hut-like structures. The best part was that we had to return from the locality and the speed limit for 4 wheelers was only 10miles/hour in that area. But then, Ishita had not noticed the speed limit and though she was driving slowly, at a speed of about 25 miles/hour, to our surprise, a policeman came with a Motorcycle and asked to stop the vehicle. As per the rule in vogue, she parked the car by the side of the road and opened her seat belt. The police, asked her why she was over speeding? After getting a satisfactory answer and the modesty in Ishita's behaviour, the Policeman took out a laptop and asked for the licence. Rachita and I were surprised to see what was happening. The policeman with all records warned Ishita and fined USD 40. Then again, we proceeded towards the beach. Manoj was extremely happy that, we escaped with a warning letter and imposition of a fine of only USD 40.

Though Ishita had a bad mood, the moment we reached the parking area of Rehoboth Beach, she and the rest of us were very thrilled. By then it was around 5 pm. We all then went to the beach after walking for only 10 minutes and Manoj & I preferred to bathe in the sea including my niece, Ruchi, who was about 8 years old. We had really good fun bathing in very low tides, shallow water and also seeing a lot of seagulls there. That beach is one of the nice beaches of the Atlantic Sea. After bathing, we were very hungry and came to the parking area. There were several beautiful restaurants and pubs around the corner, having all varieties of food from different parts of the world. We chose to have Mexican food with a glass of beer. After finishing our food, we started our return journey. On the return journey, Manoj drove the car and we reached home at around 11 pm. It was overall a very enjoyable day. On Monday, Manoj went to the office and we walked around the nearby places and rest of the time, chilled at home.

The next day, Rachita, Ishita, and I went to Washington DC, by local train, which only took 30 minutes to get us there. We then walked to the Lincoln memorial first and also visited the World War II Memorial and the Washington Monument. That whole area was a tourist area and very well maintained with beautiful lush green grass. We then had food in a nearby kiosk and took a little rest after walking a lot. Then, we walked to the great landmark named 'The Smithsonian Institution' in DC. Incidentally, 'The Smithsonian Institution' is the largest museum, education, and research complex, with 19 museums and many other landmark complexes. First, we went to National Air and Space Museum. It was such an amazing place with around 17,000 space aircraft in its collection. The majority of them were from the Apollo Moon landing mission. More than 400 objects related specifically to the first successful lunar landing mission, Apollo-11. A section of Apollo -11 objects and their description were also viewable in this grouping. After completing this visit, we visited the 'National Museum of Natural History'. It was a very huge museum and even difficult to cover the whole area. But it was a very nice experience to know that it had a collection of over 145 million specimens of plants, animals, fossils, minerals, rocks, meteorites, human remains, and cultural artefacts. It is the museum with the largest collection in the world. We were amazed to see the ancient dinosaur, elephants, and up to a hundred different butterflies. We also saw different types of fossils and even the aquarium area had large numbers of sea animals. It was a fantastic place not only to spend quality time but also to acquire knowledge. It was so huge and fascinating that it would have taken a whole day to see everything in detail.

It was already around 6 pm and Ishita, said we would leave that place and go to another interesting place. We could not comprehend and walked with her and went to another building. She bought tickets for the I-MAX theatre and we went inside. It was a one-hour programme and was related to space shuttles. While entering the hall, we were given black 3D spectacles and we saw the movie. We felt as if the sky and other objects are simply coming and touching us. It was an unforgettable experience to visit the 'I-MAX'. At around 7 pm, we started from the Smithsonian area. It was virtually impossible to see all the museums and galleries in that area. We then boarded the train and came back from there and reached home at around 8:30 pm. We were tired by that time and Manoj was back home by then and anxiously waiting for us. The moment we reached home, he offered with a 'Stella Artois' beer, which I took for the first time. I was so tired that gulped few pints and got refreshed. We all then had our dinner, which Manoj had prepared and enjoyed thoroughly.

Chapter 7:

Surprises, Ostriches, and Gigantic Waterfalls

On that day, when we had gone to visit Washington DC along with Ishita, Manoj had done some paperwork, during our absence. The next day, we got up late in the morning and chilled during the first half of the day. Post lunch, we again went to the 'RIO' area, which was very near and a place of enjoyment. We came back around 6 pm and Manoj reached home around 6:30 pm. While having tea, he handed over certain papers, which he had prepared the previous day, and gave us a surprise. He then started explaining about a Canada trip, the coming week. It was Wednesday that he gave us the papers and it was nothing, but the related papers for obtaining a visa for Canada. That evening Manoj & Ishita explained to us how to reach the Canadian Visa centre in Washington DC. It became easier for us to understand, as because, we had been to DC with Ishita 2 days back. Rachita and I kept the papers ready and the next morning Ishita dropped us near the metro station in her car and she further explained to us right from booking tickets in the metro for the train to all details on how to reach the Canadian visa office.

We started at around 8 am and reached the visa office around 9:30 am. We submitted our passports and related papers around 10:30 am at the counter. The lady sitting at the counter asked us a few questions and told us to come around 2 pm to check upon our visas. Since we had sufficient time, we walked through the market and did some usual window shopping. Around 12:30, we felt hungry and went to a nearby restaurant and had our lunch. That day, the visa was very important for us but not the lunch. However, we had a quick lunch and started walking towards the visa office. We reached there around 2 pm and anxiously waited, for the counter to open. The counter opened, sharp at 2:30 pm and we kept our fingers crossed. Our names were announced at around 2:45 pm and we had butterflies in the stomach. When we opened our packet, we found that our visas for Canada have been granted for 3 months. We were very happy and hugged each other. We then started our journey towards home and reached around 5 pm. Ishita was waiting, with certain preparation done for the travel to Canada on Saturday. She was extremely excited about our visa and then we started our full-fledged preparation on the next day, i.e., Friday for a 10 days' trip to Canada.

On Saturday morning, we kept several foodstuffs with beer, etc., in a big icebox and kept them in the car along with our luggage. As the vehicle was a 7-seater huge SUV, there was enough space and we started taking the name of "GOD" with a big bang. It was around 11 am, we started from home. Manoj was driving the car and I was sitting in the front seat. The voice-activated GPS was on and we started moving on the highway. We were heading towards Niagara Falls, which was about 400 miles away. We had our food on the way and went to the restroom. Since it was our debut visit to the USA, the restroom concept was very new for us. We took a road by the side of the highway and maybe after 1 mile, it was there. It had benches, toilets, refreshments, etc. We took a little rest and then proceeded. It was very typical of the USA that such free restrooms were available by the side of the highway, which I had not seen earlier in my life, even in Europe. From that place, Ishita started driving on the highway and Manoj took a rest in the back seat. I was still in the front seat, having the habit of "not even dozing" during the drive. I was playing some music and was gossiping with Ishita, to keep her alert.

We knew, Niagara Falls is situated at the international boundary between the USA and Canada. On the USA side, Niagara Falls is in the Buffalo Metropolitan area and the state of New York. We chose to stop before the international border and reached around 7 pm at the hotel which Manoj had booked earlier. The next morning, we saw Niagara Falls and enjoyed the panoramic view. Then, we crossed the border and went to the Canadian side, which was Ontario. Niagara Falls is in a city in Ontario and is situated on the western bank of the Niagara River. It is the Golden Horseshoe region of Southern Ontario.

Our prime aim was to see and enjoy Niagara Falls in the evening and we had the whole day to us. Manoj had also booked the hotel near Niagara. So, we travelled further and went to the Toronto Zoo. The uniqueness of the zoo was that, one could take one's vehicle and give a declaration or else, could take the vehicle of the zoo by paying additional money in addition to the ticket. The distance was around 100 miles and we reached the zoo within an hour and a half. The time was around 11 am. We preferred to take our vehicle inside the zoo with full glass closed, which was the rule, because of the wild animals and birds left free in the majority area of the zoo. It was the biggest zoo in Canada and the zoo was divided into 7 geographical zones. Some animals were displayed indoor, but the majority of animals were outdoors in what would be their natural environment. It also had a Kids Zoo, Waterside Theatre, etc. We saw the tigers, lions, and ostriches from very close proximity. Even the ostriches came near our car window panes and were touching their beak to the window glass panes, which was very thrilling. After having spent about 2 hours, we returned to Niagara again, where we had our hotel booking. We had our lunch on the way and checked into the hotel around 3:30 pm and the best part was that Niagara Falls was only at a distance of 10 minutes from our hotel.

We went to Niagara at around 5 pm. It had a beautiful ambience and symphony was going on around that place, and in the whole area, people were enjoying in different ways. There was a beautiful landscape with a beautiful garden and lush green grass. Manoj asked us to go for a ride on the small cruise (boat) to go to the nearest point of Niagara Falls on the river Niagara. The name of the tour was called "Maid of the mist". We were provided with a raincoat and we boarded the small cruise or we can call it a boat, as the top was open. The total to and from journey duration was around one hour. The waves of the river and the rocking boat were giving a different experience. The nearer we went to the Falls, the more the mist was visible. The boat finally took us to the nearest point of Niagara Falls where we got drenched, even with the raincoats on. It was just an amazing experience, to see Niagara Falls from a very close distance and at the same time enjoying the mist generated from the waterfall.

We then climbed up the steps and came to the top of the garden area, from where most of the people were enjoying the sight of Niagara Falls. The whole area was a happening place, having the symphony with a grand orchestra and the pump & gange happening on that day. It was more vibrant on that day, as was because it was 4TH of July 2007. Incidentally, 4th July was the Independence Day of the USA and the Independence Day of Canada is on 1st July and hence, the whole week was being celebrated at Niagara. All the big crowd and activities were happening because of that. We then had a variety of food from different kiosks and relaxed on the lawn of the garden. There was a scheduled firework and lights show after the sunset. As it was summer in the USA & Canada, the sunset started after 9 pm. Then the fireworks started with different colours and there was a laser light falling on Niagara Falls with beautiful music in the background. It was an unbelievable sight which I can never forget. However, all the beautiful things are a joy for ever, but we were not feeling like coming back from such an ambience. Of course, most of the activities got over by 11pm and we started towards our hotel.

The next day we checked out from the hotel at Niagara and proceeded to Toronto, where, we had a hotel booking. I had contacted one of my friends Harihar, who lived in Toronto. He was in fact in constant communication with me, as to when we would reach Toronto. On that day, Manoj had some official job in a place about 40 miles from Toronto and he went for his job, the moment we checked into the hotel. My friend Harihar reached around 11 am in our hotel with his SUV and said he is at our disposal for the whole day and would show us all important places. The first place that we went to was C N Tower (Canadian National Tower). Harihar dropped us there and said, he would come after an hour since he had some work. We then went near the C N Tower and after seeing the long queue for going to the top of the tower, we got scared. But we were determined to climb the tower as that was the tallest tower in the world in 2007. We were very thrilled right from the beginning that, we would be climbing the tallest tower having a height of 533.3 metres. The tower had remained the tallest tower for 32 years. It was a signature icon of the Toronto skyline and attracted more than a million tourists annually. The most thrilling part of the tower was the elevator speed. We reached the top within a minute. The speed of the elevator was 22 Km/Hour, which was mind-boggling. At the top, the view of Toronto city was very beautiful. Another, amazing feature of the tower was that the floor of the top deck was made of glass and one can see to the bottom, which was also scary to some extent, for me. But the children of Ishita were enjoying on the glass floor and I took lot of photographs of them and the overall view of Toronto.

After spending ample time at the top of the tower, we came down and by then, Harihar had already arrived. He then took us to several parts of Toronto city, including the University of Toronto. The ancient buildings of the University, which were established in 1827, were well maintained. The first institute of Toronto University was King's College. After having a round in the university, we went to the Toronto Harbour. It was a beautiful sight, which is located on the North shore of Lake Ontario. It is a natural harbour. We went for a boat ride for an hour and enjoyed it thoroughly. After coming back to the harbour, we had lunch and spent some quality time there. I and Harihar had shared all the old stories of our college time in REC, Rourkela (Presently NIT, Rourkela). Harihar then dropped us in the hotel and invited us for dinner at his house. It was around 6 pm that we reached the hotel and at the same time Manoj was also back. Rachita and I went for dinner, but others opted to relax at the hotel. Harihar dropped us in the hotel at around 10 pm after dinner. We were extremely delighted to meet a friend in Toronto whose hospitality for the whole day was unparalleled.

The next morning, we all started for Montreal, around 10 am. The journey was around 5 hours and 30 minutes and the road was just great. On our way, we had lunch and at around 5 pm we reached Montreal. We checked into the hotel and took a rest that evening. The next morning, we went to the Olympic stadium in Montreal. It was the biggest stadium that I had ever seen. After visiting the stadium, we proceeded towards the marketplace, which was located in the heart of downtown. It was Crescent Street, which was the most action-packed street attracting both locals and visitors like us. The people were dressed in colourful apparel and were enjoying in the streets. We sat in a horse-driven cart, which was very enjoyable. The whole day we enjoyed ourselves in that area only and then went to the old Montreal area and saw the monumental and historical buildings. It was a unique experience to walk through the streets of old Montreal.

That night, we stayed back in our hotel and the next day started for Quebec City. The distance was around 160 miles. We travelled very leisurely enjoying the beauty of the roadside mountains enroute to Quebec. We reached Quebec City at around 4 pm. Our hotel was situated in the new downtown area. The city is at a higher elevation. It was situated on the bank of Saint Lawrence River in Canada's French-speaking area. The old city area was a beautiful place with stone buildings and narrow streets. The cobblestone streets were lined with bistros and boutiques. We had several varieties of food and took a lot of photographs in the old town area, which was the centre of attraction. We then went near a castle-like structured hotel named 'Chateau Frontenac', which was very famous and the world's most photographed hotel, because of the architecture and the lighting at night. After nightfall, we took several photographs of the castle-style hotel with its turrets, copper roof-top, and dominance of the architecture, in the skyline of the city, which is still a good memory for us.

The climate at Quebec was serene and just awesome. The next morning after breakfast, we started for a nearby waterfall named ''Montmorency Falls' which was one of the largest waters falls in Canada. There was a staircase that allowed us to view the falls from several different perspectives. A suspension bridge over the crest of the fall provided access to both sides of the adjacent park. The typical thing about the waterfall was that it was giving a yellow glow due to the high iron content in the water. Surprisingly, when I read about the water fall's history and specification, on a display board near the fall, I came to know that it was almost 100 feet taller than Niagara Falls. The total height of the waterfall is 272 feet high, as against Niagara Falls' height of 167 feet.

While returning from the fall, we had lunch and then saw a big hillock with a garden. Since we had the voice-activated GPS, we ventured to go to that secluded area for a different experience. Surprisingly we arrived at a beautiful place where the area was full of strawberry orchards and farming was going on, on a big scale. First time in my life, I saw a strawberry orchard. The farming families living there were very warm-hearted. They were sitting and having a beer and two guys out of them, were doing acrobatics on their bikes. That was an amazing sight. All of them were very excited and we developed a friendship with them. They told us, not only to pluck strawberry and eat but also, asked us to take away, as much as we can. It was very interesting to pluck strawberry and eat it then and there. We had good fun and thanked them all and came to our hotel with packets of strawberry. Since we had taken a suite in the hotel, it was provided with a refrigerator and a furnished kitchen. We ate enough strawberries and kept the remaining in the fridge for the next day.

Since Quebec City was our last destination in Canada, the next morning we went shopping and bought many souvenirs for our family and friends. Rachita and her sister Ishita, did a lot of shopping and spent their time. I and Manoj went to a beer parlour in the narrow inclined old streets of Quebec and had a couple of beers in a beautiful ambience under the big umbrellas. Next, we wanted to have the experience of dog sledding in old Quebec City. But, because of summer, dog sledding was not in service, as it is required to have ice all around. One gentleman suggested and explained in our hotel that, we can see the dogs, where and how they are kept during summer. We, then proceeded to the lower town area and with a cable car went up the hill to see the dogs, where they are kept in the cannel. The place is called 'Terrassa Dufferin'. There were hundreds of dogs in open areas and channels, well-fed and well-maintained by a few young girls. Those girls were in charge of taking care of those dogs, who would be used for dog sledding in winter. It was a unique experience, not only to see the healthy dogs, but also it was very interesting to talk to the caretaker girls. From the top, the other side of the cable car junction was full of hills and forest. It was a beautiful sight. After having spent a couple of hours there, we again came downhill by the same cable car.

We reached our hotel around 7 pm and were tired and hungry. We ordered some snacks immediately and then ordered our dinner to our room and had it, while discussing the whole experience of around 10 days trip to Canada, right from Niagara to Quebec. Discussing every event late into the night, was very enjoyable, as the next day was the commencement day of our return journey. It was around 920 km (around 580 miles) from Quebec to the USA border near Niagara that we would drive. The drive was around 9 hours. We had no plan to visit any tourist spots in our return journey, as we had thoroughly enjoyed the 10 days trip and stayed right from Niagara, Toronto, Montreal, and finally Quebec.

The next morning, we started our return journey leisurely around 11 am. Manoj deliberately gave the command to his GPS for a route up to the Canada border to commute in the road without toll gates. It means that he intended to show us the countryside of Canada, which was no doubt a longer route by an hour than the other route. He had a plan to have a stopover near the border and we reached there at around 9.30 pm. After a long drive, we stayed in a hotel named 'Holiday Inn'. The next morning, we stated for the USA. At the border, we went to the duty-free shop and did some shopping. We bought souvenirs, perfumes, etc., and I bought a 'Bushnell' make set of binoculars, which I correctly remember cost me 75 Canadian Dollars. I had a long desire to have good binoculars, which I purchased there. I still possess it and take it along whenever I go to any jungle or a scenic place. After a good shopping spree at the duty-free shop, we started for home to Gaithersburg. The distance was around 700 km (450 miles). We leisurely travelled and reached home around 8 pm.

When we reached home, we found that on the 1st floor, one portion was flooded with water. Manoj and we all started searching for the source of the water leakage. It was found later that the water was dripping from a connection in the bathroom, which was worked upon by an Iranian plumber named Ali before we had started for our journey to Canada. We somehow plugged the leakage and cleaned everything, including the wet carpets. It was a terrible night for all of us and that day we slept at about 2 am. Plummer Ali came the next day and was very apologetic and immediately fixed it.

The next day, we got up late and simply chilled for the whole day. The next day was a Saturday and one of Manoj's friends named Sastry had invited us for dinner. Around 6:30 pm we reached his house and were amazed to see his huge house. There was a swimming pool, a lift for going to the upper floor, and a total of 3 Mercedes Benz vehicles, 2 cars, and one SUV. He had also invited some of his family friends. He was a big shot, owning a software company. He was basically a Mining Engineer and was working for Coal India Ltd, as a Deputy Manager and had migrated to the USA after quitting his job. I was then a Deputy General Manager and working for Steel Authority of India Ltd. He was taking a keen interest in me as he had also served as a Public Sector Undertaking (PSU) in India like me and we had several conversations about the PSU status in India. He was a very smart and jovial person. He served us good wine and several types of snacks and finally dinner. I was waiting for some non-vegetarian dish and it never came. Finally, I came to know that Mr. Sastry's family was purely vegetarian.

We had 3 more days left in the USA and it was not sinking into me that we were coming back to India after a fantastic stay for such a long time. I was feeling as if I was in a dream and not in a mood to come back. However, as we had three days in hand, we did not travel much. One day we went to the nearby marketplace for shopping, which was a place of hundreds of branded shops with factory outlets. It was a great marketing place in Hagerstown, which is also the commercial and industrial hub for a greater Tri-State area that includes a large area of western Maryland, a significant portion of South-Central Pennsylvania, and the Eastern Panhandle of West Virginia. Hagerstown is also referred to as "The Hub City". It attracts visitors from all nearby states and we also had real fun buying stuff from there.

The same evening, we again went to Rio, to a pub which was also an eating joint. Manoj and I tried several varieties of "Draught beer" on that day. After dinner, we preferred walking by the side of the lake. It was a beautiful evening. The next day Rachita and Ishita wanted to go shopping again and during that period Manoj wanted to give a surprise. He simply drove and we reached the Baltimore harbour area. We moved to the harbour side for some time and enjoyed the sea breeze. Then, he took me to a place where we saw pole dance and it was full of acrobatics and was very fascinating. I saw that for the first time and had a unique experience.

We had our return flight after 2 days. Since there was a lot of shopping done during the stay, it was a difficult task for us, packing the baggage. The next morning, we started packing and it took almost more than a day. It was Wednesday and both Ishita and Manoj came to drop us at Dallas airport, which was only a 45 minutes' drive from their house. Our flight was at 1 pm and we reached the airport around 10 am. Since it was our first visit to the USA and we had a lot of luggage, it was overweight and we had to pay 50 USD extra for the luggage. After all formalities, we checked in and I thought of buying 2 litres of alcohol, as unlike other duty-free shops in any airport which was cheaper in the Dallas duty-free shop.

We then boarded the flight and found that it was American Airlines operated by Swiss Air. The flight took off and we were in grief. On board, we found most of the crew members were male instead of female. On the top of it, all the males were with shaved heads. Probably, that was then the style in vogue. One more problem in the aircraft was that nothing was free in the aircraft including water. I bought a can of beer for 5 USD in the aircraft and drank it. The return journey was not that enjoyable as we were thinking of our routine work after going back home and the excitement had dampened. Of course, we were returning with beautiful memories. It was almost 8 hours flight and we reached Zurich at 5 am Swiss time. We did not have a good sleep and our next flight was at noon from Zurich to Mumbai, India. During our security check to go to another terminal, the security personnel was checking, if anybody is carrying liquid. To my bad luck, I was carrying 2 bottles of whisky. The security personnel asked me to throw the 2 litres of alcohol, that I had brought in the Dallas Airport. It was very disappointing for me and I could not say anything. After the formalities were completed, we went to the waiting area of the airport. However, in Zurich airport, I again went to the duty-free shop and bought 2 more bottles of alcohol. I saw Bollywood actor Kunal Kapoor and was extremely thrilled. I forgot all the misery and tiredness, just by seeing him. To our luck, he boarded the same flight from Zurich to Mumbai. We reached Mumbai at around 4 pm. We were a bit apprehensive about our baggage and came to Green Channel. One of the lady custom officers asked us several questions and then let us go. We were very happy and came out of the airport.

Chapter 8:

Daughters' Achievement, Silver Jubilee Celebration & Giant Water Lilies

When we returned from USA to Mumbai, India in July 2007, our elder daughter, Anisha, was studying 2nd year MSW in Tata Institute of Social Sciences (TISS) and was then in Mumbai. She came to the airport to receive us, along with one of her friends. We were extremely happy to see her. We then boarded the taxi and went to a guest house, very near to her hostel. We opened all gifts and articles that we had brought from the USA. Anisha took her share and was very happy. We stayed for a day in Mumbai, took a rest and the next day we came to Rourkela by train.

Returning home after about 40 days felt overwhelming. My mother-in-law was taking care of our younger daughter Anooja at our home, during our long absence. Both were staring at us for a moment when we reached home and then I hugged Anooja, which was a different nostalgic experience. At that time Anooja was in class XI and busy preparing for her +2 examinations. She was also preparing for the Law entrance examination simultaneously, by taking an online tutorial. As during those days, there was no provision of class room coaching of Law Entrance Examination at Rourkela. Hence, after Anooja's +2 examination in Commerce, she went to Bhubaneswar for a month for class room coaching of Law.

The most problematic part, then was, different good law colleges had different dates for their entrance examinations in those days and some dates were getting clashed. Hence, appearing for all entrance examinations was virtually impossible. Fortunately, Government of India declared in 2008 that, there shall be only one entrance examination for all National Law universities of India and named it as "Common law admission test", CLAT. At that time there were some 14 good law colleges in India.

2008 was a land mark year as CLAT started that year and Anooja was supposed to appear for the CLAT examination, as the first batch and she had also simultaneously appeared for +2 Commerce. At the same time my elder daughter Anisha, was also going to finish her Masters from TISS and sit for several Campus interviews. As Anisha was completing her Masters and her Convocation was scheduled on 4th July 2008, we had also made a programme to attend it. Accordingly, we advised Anooja to opt for CLAT examination centre at Mumbai, as the date of examination of CLAT was on 8th of July. By then, Anooja's +2 results were out and she scored 92% in Commerce. We were very happy and were quite sure, if she does not get through in CLAT, she would get in some good law college like Govt. Law College, Mumbai, Indian Law School, Pune, etc., as those colleges were taking students on mark's basis. She had also applied for Symbiosis Law, which was having a different examination.

Accordingly, we had booked ticket in train for all 3 of us to go to Mumbai on 2nd July, so that we would reach Mumbai on the 3rd and attend Anisha's Convocation at TIIS on 4th July. About 3 days before our departure from Rourkela, Anisha informed that their convocation has been postponed, as the Chief guest had rescheduled his programme. The chief guest was Lord Megnad Desai, from the London School of Economics. At that moment, we did not have any option and proceeded to Mumbai on 2nd July. Though, we would not attend

Anisha's convocation, Anooja got a bit time for her preparation in Mumbai. We also enjoyed ourselves a bit by going to different good eating joints and visiting places, which Anisha knew quite well, being in Mumbai for 2 years. Anooja appeared her examination of CLAT on 8th July and said that she did well. We all kept our fingers crossed for her results.

By then, Anisha had already got a job through Campus interview and was supposed to join on the 10th of July in her new company. Her new role was in the CSR part of a corporate house in Mumbai. Anisha was very excited about it and also showed us her office location on 8th July, after Anooja's Common Law Admission Test (CLAT) examination was over. Anisha was smart enough to look for her house and her flat partner, whose name was also Anooja. We were not much worried about her, as she was capable of taking care of herself.

On 10th, all 3 of us came back to Rourkela and were waiting for the CLAT results to be out. It was her first priority to join any National Law School, instead of ILS or GLC, etc. Fortunately, we got a telephonic call from 'Ram Manohar Lohia National Law University' (RMLNLU), Lucknow, saying that, as per her rank in CLAT, she has got a seat in RMLNLU and that day only it was uploaded in their college web site. Listening to the good news, we were in the seventh heaven. The email correspondence started and we got a seat confirmed. We proceeded to Lucknow on 28th of July, 2008, for her admission. Unfortunately, there was no direct train from Rourkela to Lucknow at that time. Hence, we had to go to Jamshedpur and then went to Lucknow by Amritsar express. We started at around 7 pm and reached at Lucknow at 3 pm on 29th July. Lucknow was a new place for us, as none of us had visited earlier. We had contacted one of our nephews, Amitav, who was a Professor in Bareilly and had a lot of contacts and connections in Lucknow. One of his PhD scholars, who lived in

Lucknow, came to the station to receive us. He had organised a decent hotel for us and helped us to a great extent.

Next morning, we went to the institute for admission. Seeing the college and the overall campus, we were astonished. The beautiful garden, the main entrance of the college with full glass panes and the guard standing to open the glass door, fascinated us. The whole building was centrally air-conditioned. We went to Professor, who was then, the in charge of the admissions and also the chief coordinator, who helped us a lot. The whole process of admission got over within 2 hours. Then we went to the hostel. The hostel was also very clean and excellently maintained. We completed the hostel formalities also, after seeing the rooms. Next day we bought all necessary articles for the hostel and saw to it that Anooja was comfortable to stay in the new environment. She continued her law and did quite well in her 5 years Integrated Law. She took special interest in Moot Court and won several awards in different institutes all over the country. She also specialised in intellectual property rights (IPR) and came out with flying colours in her 5 years Integrated Law final examination in 2013. She did not opt to sit in any Campus interview and with her own effort, got a decent job in a Legal IPR firm at Gurugram.

Coming to another aspect of life, as we were married in 1984, in 2009 we were completing our 25 years of marriage (Silver Jubilee). I had a great plan of going to a place abroad for a week. In 2001, I had seen a movie titled "Albela", starring Govinda, Aishwariya Rai, and Namrata Shirodkar. The movie was shot in Mauritius, which had triggered my fascination to go to Mauritius for my silver jubilee marriage anniversary. I tried to plan it in 2009 May/June. But then my father was not well and we could not execute the plan. We therefore dropped the programme in 2009 and decided to go in 2010.

Deciding to go to Mauritius in 2010, eventually became a nice decision, as that year our salary revision was done and we had a substantial salary hike, which was due from 2007. It was a wage revision and the biggest jump ever in salary, which we got it in 2010, with a special pay also called Performance Related Pay (PRP). We got the arrear from 2007 also, which was a handsome amount and it was a great relief for us.

When we decided to go to Mauritius, we had sufficient money in hand, for the first time. Incidentally, at that time also there was no reputed travel agent at Rourkela, who could organise a foreign tour. Hence, I did not have any option but to go to Bhubaneswar for enquiry and found that M/s SOTC is organising tour for Mauritius. I went to Bhubaneswar in February '2010 and discussed with M/s SOTC in detail and fixed up a programme for 6 nights and 7 days in May 2010. I paid them advance immediately and paid rest of the amount before 45 days of the journey.

We chose 3 days conducted tour organised by M/s SOTC and remaining 3 days we wanted to chill and be of our own out of our total 6 nights and 7 days' tour. Our flight was scheduled from Mumbai and we chose to go by Air Mauritius. From Rourkela we first went to Bhubaneswar by train and then flew to Mumbai. We stayed in a guesthouse at Andheri east. Our daughter, Anisha, immediately came to the Andheri guesthouse and spent time with us. We did some shopping with her for our travel. Next day was our scheduled travel to Mauritius and it was at 3 in the morning. Because of the odd departure timing, we reached the international airport at 11 pm. We finished all our formalities and were ready in the departure isle at 1 am and waited there for 2 hours. Our flight departed exactly at 3 am. It was a beautiful flight and the crew members were very courteous. It was an all-female crew. The food and alcoholic beverages served in the flight were awesome. We had a great time in the flight of about 6 hours. We obviously had not slept that night and had a nap only for about 2 hours in the flight itself.

We landed at Mauritius International Airport at around 7:30 am (Mauritius time). The best part was that, for Indians, there was no requirement of pre-approved Visa and we got it only on arrival. Like previous tours, one gentleman was waiting for us with a plaque card. We were glad to see him and he escorted us to the vehicle. We travelled around 1 hour and reached our hotel. The journey from the airport to the hotel was just great with curvilinear roads and full of greenery. Most of the stretch was full of sugarcane plants on both sides of the road. When we reached the hotel, there was a nice reception with a flower bud and a glass of fresh fruit juice. It was a beautiful and cosy hotel named 'Casuarina Resort and Spa'. The driver of the vehicle had delivered to us all the vouchers for 3 days conducted tour while getting down from the vehicle.

The entrance of the hotel had a beautiful garden, full of flowers. We were surprised to see such flowers, as we compared Mauritius's climate with the scorching heat of summer in India, during that time. In fact, Mauritius is an Island of East Africa and situated in the Southern Hemisphere. Hence, the climate is almost opposite to that of India. The winter starts from May up to October and the climate was beautiful as we went to Mauritius in May. The maximum temperature was 27 degrees Centigrade and was extremely pleasant. We freshened up and had our lunch and then took rest as we had not slept properly the previous night. In the evening, we went round the hotel and explored all the facilities there. We found a spa, two swimming pools, one pool side bar and two more bars with a beautiful restaurant. The whole hotel was full of cottages and beautiful garden all around. We also walked in the street to explore the sea and some stores for emergency purchase.

Every evening at 7 pm they had a buffet dinner with live band. They also served one complementary alcoholic beverage and the subsequent drink, we had to order. It was an amazing experience on the very first day to have dinner with the live band in attendance. We, being music lovers, also requested them to sing some numbers and they sang. We were one of the last couples to leave the place after the band was over. We developed a rapport with the lead singer, who was wearing a hat while singing.

The next morning, a vehicle arrived at around 10 am as per schedule, with a young lady as our tour guide. That was the first day of our conducted tour and they took us to a place which was the remains of a volcano having multi coloured sand. The place was situated in Chamarel, which is a small village. The road leading to that place was full of sugarcane plantation. We climbed up the observation deck outpost and enjoyed the incredible view of the coloured sand. There were different types of coloured rocks and it was a very nice sight. The place was also called 7 coloured earth, as the colour of stones were of 7 types. Our next trip was to 'The Trou Aux Cerfs' also known as Murr's Volcano, a dormant volcano. It is one of the most famous natural tourist attractions. The dormant volcano was surrounded by lush green trees and grass, which was something unique to see. The size of the volcano was huge, around 605 meters above mean sea level with a diameter of 350 meters and depth of about 85 meters.

Our next and last trip on that day, was to a botanical garden named 'Sir Seewoosagar Ramgoolam Botanical Garden'. It was near the capital 'Port Louis' and is the oldest botanical garden in the Southern Hemisphere. It was very famous for its long and huge pond of giant water lilies. In addition to giant water lilies, the garden was full of 85 varieties of palms from Central America, Asia and Africa. The uniqueness of the lily was the leaf, rather than the size and beauty of the flower itself. The leaves were so big that the birds sitting on the top of the leaf for eating insects, were looking miniature, as compared to the leaf. To have a feel of the size, we also took photograph of the leaf with a bird sitting on it.

After that day's visit we came back to the hotel around 6 pm. After the day-long trip, we were tired and after taking bit rest, we went for the dinner. As usual the rock band was in attendance and we were enjoying the music along with our food and drinks. All our fatigue went away with the relaxed atmosphere.

The next day, the whole day was packed with a different kind of tour to go to a waterfall which was situated in an island. It was the "Grand River South East" trip. We went to the waterfall by a speed boat and the journey time was around an hour. It was an amazing journey to the waterfall by the speed boat, navigating in the deep water and breezy climate. We went near the waterfall and got a feeling of "Maid of the mist" of Niagara Falls. Rather, in addition to that, it was full of lush green mountains and forest. We were surprised by the drastic change of scenery as the colour of the water changes from turquoise blue to green, surrounded by a vast area of verdant trees. The huge wall of basalt rock allowed us to discern the formation of a totally different atmosphere in the area. As we reached the farthest corner, we were mesmerized by the gushing waterfall which was simply spectacular. After enjoying the beauty of waterfall, we got down from the speed boat, relaxed and chilled in the sand. The climate was very nice and I bathed in the river and finally we took several photographs there. There were beautiful restaurants and one can have food of their choice. There were several tourists from all over the globe. I enjoyed the beer while bathing in the shallow water and we then had Chinese food. It was a great moment spending the whole day in such a lovely place.

We reached the hotel at around 6:30 pm and as usual had our dinner a bit late on that day, in the same place with the live band. The next day was our 3rd day of the conducted tour. We had chosen that day for the water sports. They took us to the 'Grand Baie' on that day. Before going, we were given many tips about our attire and the do's and don'ts. Before we reached the sea, they stopped us and we made the tickets and could buy snacks etc. We packed our bags with sufficient drinking water, food etc., as nothing would be available in the sea shore, to keep the sea beach clean. Once we reached to the shore, we first went for Para sailing. It was the first experience in our life, as we had not ventured that in 1998 during Pattaya trip in Thailand. Two people could go together for para sailing, which we had chosen to go for. Initially, there was a mixed feeling of fear and excitement. But we ventured to go for it and enjoyed to a great extent, which was very thrilling. Our next venture was, snorkelling. With a speed boat we were taken further into the deep sea. We found, there was a big platform in the middle of the sea, which was the snorkelling platform. Rachita refused to take that trip and I went for it. I was given full oxygen mask and was dropped with a guide into the sea. The depth of the sea was more than 20 feet in that place and I could see several types of fishes and small sea animals. All the other people, who were inside the sea were looking very tiny in size. I had a unique experience. But I came out from the sea after 10 minutes, though the allowable time was 30 minutes, as it was a bit scary for me. We then came to the shore by the speed boat and chilled in the shore.

We had a great time that day. Our next trip was 'Mangal Mahadev' which is a 33 meters' tall sculpture of Lord Shiva. It was a nice place for all tourists. We worshiped there and enjoyed that place. Then from there, we proceeded to the harbour in Port Louis. It was the port of Mauritius for all business, as it is an island and the mode of transport was primarily through water in the sea. It was a beautiful sight with different types of ships. That was our last point of the 3 days conducted tour.

We had kept 3 days in hand to enjoy on our own way and wanted to do everything very leisurely. The next day after breakfast, we asked in the reception counter about the facilities given by the hotel in their adjacent private beach. They explained every aspect and we were given separate towels from the hotel to go to the sea beach. At around 11 am, with lot of fruits, cold drinks etc., we went to the private beach of the hotel. There were several large umbrellas and leaning chairs with life guards. We were fascinated by the sea beach and the facilities. There were very few tourists out there and we could really enjoy the day. Whole day we took bath in the clear shallow water with white sand. We then relaxed on the leaning chairs and I was having fruits and cold drinks. We came back at around 4 pm from the beach, on the first day. After coming back, I swam in the swimming pool of the hotel and finally went to the room at 6 pm. On the first day, we could discover that a glass boat goes into the deep sea in their private beach, for their guests, which was complementary at particular hours. The timing was from 10am to 11am and 3pm to 4pm and at other times, it was chargeable.

The next day, we got ready a bit early and availed the morning free ride in the glass boat to see the coral and fishes. We were extremely thrilled to see the coral and the fishes and the ride lasted for a duration of more than one hour. Tough we had been to Pattaya Coral islands, in Thailand, way back in 1998, we had not been able to see any proper coral. So, the coral in Pattaya and Mauritius were distinctively different. The experience of coral in Mauritius was absolutely fascinating. We came back to the shore and again relaxed like the previous day. The next day also we did the same thing except for the complementary boat ride and thoroughly relaxed and chilled for 3 days. The overall experience of 7 days in Mauritius was just great and the cool and serene climate further enhanced our enjoyment.

After spending a week in Mauritius, we came to Mumbai with unforgettable memories. We stayed only for a day at Mumbai and spent some time with our daughter Anisha. Then, we came to Rourkela and continued with our normal life of the day-to-day activities, attending the same old environment of the steel plant. It was the month of May and after having spent such a beautiful time in Mauritius with a maximum temperature of 28 deg. Centigrade, it was just horrible at Rourkela with a temperature of around 44 degrees Centigrade. It took a while for us to adjust at Rourkela, after such a wonderful time at Mauritius.

Chapter 9:

A Snow-White Europe and the 12 Travellers

The next year after our Mauritius trip, I was still thinking of going to Europe with my wife. It was very surprising and interesting that, in January '2011, I discovered a franchise office of the world-famous travel agent, M/s Cox and Kings, which has opened its office at Rourkela. One evening, I simply rushed in and enquired about their different international tour programmes. They were found to be very professional. I came home happily and discussed with Rachita about all their tours. Rachita, always had a desire to visit different parts of Europe, though she had gone once to Switzerland with me.

We finally had to save money for a Europe trip and planned one in 2012 June, during the summer holidays of her school. At that time, I chose a conducted tour with major places like London, Paris, Belgium, Italy and the Netherlands for 12 days. The cost of the package was Rs. 1,20,000/- per person in twin sharing basis. The cost included, airfare, stay in 3-star hotel, and all tours in Europe. We found it to be very suitable for us. In fact, I paid Rs. 50,000/- advance in the month of January 2012, as our scheduled trip was in June 2012.

The very next day, my boss called me to his room and said, there is a training programme on Slab Caster at Germany and Poland. I asked him the time and duration, and found that it might coincide with my Europe plan with Rachita. I had a mixed feeling, as I had promised Rachita for the programme and had paid an advance of Rs, 50,000/-, which was a substantial amount for me. We again had a lot of discussion at home with everybody. But to my surprise, Rachita, encouraged me to go for one-month training, which was a company sponsored programme.

I was really confused and finally decided to go for the company sponsored programme. Accordingly, I appraised by boss about my decision. The very next day, I went to M/s Cox and Kings office and told my decision about the reason of cancellation of programme. They were a bit upset, but my decision was final and the only issue was the refund of Rs. 50,000. M/s Cox and Kings said, they can't refund the money and at best can keep it pending for my future travel, which they could adjust on a later date. The second alternative that they gave was that it can be transferred to any of my friend or relative, who would travel abroad through Cox and Kings.

After knowing, that decision from Cox and kings, I was a bit relaxed. I was just waiting for our sponsored training trip by my company, to commence. In the meantime, one of my friends, called me and asked about Cox and Kings tours and their professionalism. As, I had read about them and eventually knew the franchise owner, Mr. Nayak, I said they are good. I initially could not know his actual purpose behind calling me. He had a plan to go to Europe with his friends and family and requested me to transfer Rs. 50,000 to his name. As he was a friend of mine, I agreed and the money was transferred to him accordingly.

In the meantime, my company sponsored trip was not getting finalised and time was passing by. Furthermore, my friend was not returning the money. Hence, my anxiety was sky high. Finally, in November 2012, I got my money back from him, though he visited Europe in June 2012.In the meantime, the training programme was approved and we got the confirmation in December 2012, that we would be travelling in February' 2013. I was a bit disappointed as the season was not the right time for visiting Europe due to heavy snow fall and low temperature. However, the training got delayed by a month and it was finalised for March '2013. Though it would be very cold during March, I was also elated that, I would be seeing a new country Poland, where probably I would not have gone as a tourist. My wife encouraged me to a great extent and said, I had always visited abroad during tourist-friendly seasons and I would never have gone in such a time to Europe for tourism. She also said that the experience would be different, as I would see snow and ice during that period.

Our company made all the arrangements for our travel in February 2013 to go to Germany and Poland. We were a group of 12 people selected for the training and I was one of the fortunate ones. We had to go to Kolkata for our Schgenin visa to German consulate. That was a very thrilling experience. We then, came back to Rourkela after the biometric test and the interview. Within a week we got the visa. We were given substantial amount of US dollar per day and many other facilities during training and the journey. Our air ticket was also booked by our company on Air Emirates. That was again a boon in disguise, as the Air Emirates flight would go through Dubai, via which, I had never travelled. On, the top of it, many of my friends said that the food would also be great in Air Emirates.

Finally, we proceeded to Kolkata and travelled to Dubai from there, as our layover was there in Dubai. We were very excited to travel in Air Emirates and boarded the flight at 6 am from Kolkata. The flight duration was around 5 hours. It was a great experience to travel by Emirates airlines. The food was just awesome and the on-board hospitality was unparalleled. We arrived in Dubai around 10:30 am Dubai time. Our next flight to Dusseldorf, Germany was scheduled at around 1 pm. We were dumfounded to see the Dubai airport with 3 terminals and the huge size of the airport, in the UAE. We arrived in terminal 1 and our next flight was from terminal 2. We had sufficient time in hand and bought some alcohol from the duty-free shop for the

Dusseldorf stay in Germany. We all went by the shuttle to terminal 2 and boarded our flight, which was again Air Emirates. Since, by then we were very tired, most of us slept in the flight, as the duration of flight was around 7 hours. We reached Dusseldorf airport at around 6 pm Germany time. It took about an hour for our immigration formalities and we came out of the airport. As it was mid-February, the temperature was around 3 degrees Centigrade and it was very cold for us. Two gentlemen were standing with a plaque card, wearing suit and tie. They were very courteous and also helped us in carrying some of our luggage.

First of all, when we were landing in Dusseldorf, I recalled the condition of Dusseldorf airport in 1996 July, when it was totally in shambles then, due to heavy fire in the airport. That was also my debut visit to Europe in 1996. However, during the visit in 2013 February, the same airport was just great, with all latest facilities in place.

Twelve of us travelled in 2 huge Mercedes Benz Mini bus and reached our hotel in Dusseldorf, which was about a half an hour distance from the airport. It was around 8:30 pm and we went to our respective rooms. Some friends, who had already gone about a week back, guided us about the place and eating joints. I chose to stay nearby the room of my friend Rakesh, who also was with us. On that day, by the time we settled in the hotel, it was 9:30 pm and the hotel did not have any provision for dinner and they had provision of only breakfast. Hence, I, Rakesh and two more went to a nearby restaurant and had some food and slept that day.

The next morning, when I woke up and opened the door of the balcony, it was extremely cold, which I did not realise as I was sleeping with my room heater on. I was also astonished to see the whole area, which was covered with snow. The cars and bikes parked by the side of the road were looking white covered with snow. It was a unique sight for me and I truly enjoyed the different chilling atmosphere in Europe, which I had never seen earlier.

However, that day, I finished my morning chores and went for the breakfast at around 8 am, as we were supposed to board the metro at 8:45 am to go for the training for the first day. I found that the dining hall was full of our friends and peers only and the outside guests were less in number. Then we came out of the main door of the hotel and gathered outside. It was such a lovely feeling to see the snow-covered cars and bikes and even the roads. We took several photographs out of excitement, as it was a totally a new experience for me.

In the hotel itself, we were delivered with local train tickets, which were valid for 24 hours, as per our contract, by M/s SMS Siemag, Germany, who had invited us for training. We were supposed to reach the head office of SMS Siemag by 9:30 am. All 12 of us after having the breakfast, went by a local metro and reached the office within 30 minutes. The chief coordinator of our training was waiting outside the office to receive us and guide us. He took us to a beautiful training room with all modern gadgets for training. For all the 12 of us, varieties of biscuits, coffee, and water was always available on the table itself.

Our training coordinator, initially gave an introductory presentation and the whole schedule for 2 weeks theoretical training. I and some others were interested in visiting different places as well, along with the training. On the very 1st day, we had different queries and all were cleared by a lady assistant attached with our training coordinator. We were given open metro ticket for 15 days, so that we can commute from place to place. We were also told about their courtesy travel and stay for us. Then, the training started and the sessions were taken by all highly knowledgeable people. I was one among few to take the training very seriously and at the same time, take the best with regard to seeing new places in and around Germany. On the second day of our training when we came out after the tea break, we found that it was snowing heavily. We were so happy to see the snow and danced in the snow out of joy. It was a thrilling experience for me and I smoked a cigarette, though I am not a smoker.

In the evening, while returning from the training, I discovered a pub and entered there with my friend Rakesh, who was a friendly guy among others. The name of the pub was "Barrel house". A middle-aged lady was the bartender cum the proprietor of the pub. I and my friend sat on the stool and ordered for tap beer as bottle or canned beer was not available. The pub had an interesting atmosphere and most of them were of higher age group and were enjoying to their brim. Most of them had tattoos on their body. Another typical thing about that pup was that, one can ask to play a song of his or her choice. It was a fantastic place to spend some time while returning from the training and going back to the hotel. That became one of our most frequently visited places, which was very near to our hotel.

The next day, I and Rakesh went directly from the training place to the main market area. We basically wanted to spend some good time and went to a huge shopping mall. After having spent half an hour Rakesh bought a perfume for his wife. We then walked through the street and were searching for an Asian restaurant and finally got one. We ordered Thai food with some whisky. We enjoyed that evening. The next day, I and Rakesh decided to open the whisky bottle that we had bought at Dubai airport. I had a bottle of "Glen Livet" and he had one "Jack Daniel". After the training, we entered the pub 'Barrel House' and had one mug of beer each and came back to the hotel. It was around 6 pm when we reached to the hotel and decided to have the whisky that we had and we fixed the time for the drink at 7:30 pm. I invited Rakesh to my room and opened the "Glen Livet". As usual, during my travel I carry a 'peg measurement' device and we decided to have 2 pegs each. We thoroughly enjoyed the drink with some fruits, as it was very cold outside. After the drink, we walked near our hotel to search for an

Indian restaurant and after a 10 minutes' walk, we could locate one. We had to wait in the queue and eventually got a table. It was a family run restaurant and the owner was from Himanchal Pradesh and incidentally my friend Rakesh also hailed from the same place. We developed a good rapport with the owner and that joint also became one of our frequent visiting places.

Having the training up to Friday and enjoying in the evening every day was real fun at Dusseldorf. On Tuesday, we found different brochures of events on different days at our hotel in Dusseldorf. But obviously we were waiting for the weekend. That Saturday, our chief training coordinator had organised a trip for us to Brussels in Belgium. After we had our breakfast, a mini bus came with a lady driver cum guide. We started for Brussels which was about 200 km and around 2 hours away. By 11:30 am we reached Brussels and visited the heart of the old town, the city's main plaza known as 'Grand Place'. Its unique architecture of its guild houses, ornately carved stone work and rich gold decoration, fascinated us. There were many hawkers, who were selling flowers and souvenirs, which was giving a further elegant look to that place. We then went to another famous land mark 'The Manneken Pis', which was a small boy urinating, popularly referred to as "The oldest citizen of Brussels". In that place, surprisingly, we met 2 of our friends, Suresh & Kishor, from Rourkela Steel Plant, who had gone to the Netherlands for some other training and they had a so come to visit Brussels. It was such a pleasant surprise for us and for them too.

Then we went to the 'Saint Michel Cathedral'. This church facade is impressive and crowned with 69 meters' tall twin towers. The beautiful interior is lavishly furnished with some outstanding glass windows. We then proceed to 'The Royal Palace' which is used by the Belgian Royal family as an official residence. The Belgian flag flown from the roof signals the sovereign presence and the ceremonial guard which took place at around 2.30 pm. There were several cultural buildings, having neo classical facades, which we could see and thoroughly enjoyed.

We then proceeded to Belgium's Royal Museum of Fine Arts, which is one of the largest and best art galleries in the world. We then went to 'Parc du Cinquantenarie' which was built to commemorate the 50th century anniversary. The front side of the area was having a beautiful garden and a water fountain. It was very pleasant and we spent some time there. Finally, we went to 'Atomium' and spent maximum time there. The nearby mini-Europe adjacent to the Atomium was amazing. The 102-meter-high steel and aluminium structure of the Atomium was designed in 1958 for the Brussel world exhibition. The structure represents a molecule of iron magnified 165 million times. We bought the ticket and went through the elevator inside the hollow structure. We can call it a "Bhul Bhulaiya" in Hindi. It was quite a unique experience to go inside the 'Atomium'. From the top of the structure, we could see the Mini-Europe. By the time we came down from the Atomium it was evening and we were extremely tired. I, along with Rakesh and another friend Dilip, sat in front of a nearby kiosk and had some snacks and enjoyed beer. Our lady guide was very courteous and was explaining everything very nicely. We then started our return journey and reached Dusseldorf at around 8.30 pm.

The next day was the 1st Sunday at Dusseldorf and I and my friend Rakesh, wanted to chill and move about the city. All other friends, went to Paris by train, the previous day, after coming back from Brussels. We did not go to Paris, as it would have been very hectic and secondly, I and Rakesh had visited Paris earlier in 1996.On Sunday morning, we got up late and after having breakfast we started moving around different parts and market places of Dusseldorf. My friend, Rakesh, was in fact trying to find out a place where we could chill in the evening with a glass of beer and watch pole dance. Post lunch, after having food in a restaurant, we started searching for a good joint, so that we could relax in the evening. Though it was hectic, we finally could get the place. We then came back to our hotel at around 6 pm and took rest for some time. Then I and Rakesh went to a good place to watch pole dance on the Sunday evening. It was a different experience to watch pole dance after 2007 and the ambience was better that I had seen earlier. The best part was, the street was full of such night clubs. A pint of beer was complimentary along with the entry fee, and there was no time limit to enjoy the evening at Dusseldorf. We thoroughly enjoyed the glittering lights of the street and the overall place. After visiting that place, we recommended it to our friends.

The next day, as usual our theoretical training started and we were truly having a learning session. At the same time, we were anxiously waiting for the weekend for relaxation and enjoyment. Even during working days, after the training, we were visiting the river side of river Rhine and also some Indian restaurant several times.

On Saturday, which I remember was 23rd of March, 2013, some of the senior executives of M/s SMS Siemag accompanied us and we all went to Amsterdam. I had initiated that visit, primarily to see the world-famous Tulip Garden near Amsterdam, which was a long pending dream for me. The reason was that the romantic scene of movie 'Silsila' was shot in that Tulip Garden and I had seen the movie in August 1981, when I had joined SAIL and was posted at Bokaro Steel Plant. I was then at the prime of my youth and those beautiful scenes of the Tulip Garden was engraved in my mind.

Eventually, during my first visit in 1996 to Amsterdam, it was in the month of July and during that period Tulip does not bloom and hence we could not visit the Tulip Garden. So, during this visit in March 2013, the garden was open for visitors. In fact, the Tulip Garden was about 40 km from Amsterdam city and the name of the place is Keukenhof, which is known as 'Garden of Europe'. It is one of the world's largest flower gardens, which is situated in the town of Lisse.

At around 10:30 am we reached Amsterdam and first took a walking tour and saw all the landmarks. As I had seen Amsterdam thoroughly in 1996, it was a repetition except for the Tulip Garden. Finally, we had lunch and were ready for the visit to the Tulip Garden. It took us about 40 minutes to reach there. We took one guide who was in her late fifties and was very smart. She took us around the green house area and also the gardens. It was such an amazing experience to see the Tulips and Orchids. We were extremely lucky, as the garden opens for only 8 weeks from mid-March to mid-May, for the general public. We took around 2 hours to visit the garden and were amazed to see such a garden. It was a life time experience, for all of us. I recapitulated the romantic song of movie 'Silsila' again, which was shot in the same Tulip Garden.

We, then came to Amsterdam and had our dinner and proceeded to Dusseldorf. After an eventful and hectic day, we reached our hotel at Dusseldorf around 10 pm and slept. The next day being a Sunday, we got up late and made a programme to Duisburg Zoo, which I had seen, during my visit in 1996. During this visit, the other friends present in 1996 were not there and my new group mates, prompted me to go there. I, Rakesh and 2 more friends, went to the zoo. The main attraction was the dolphin show and whale show in that zoo. But then, the whale show was permanently closed and dolphin show was closed on Sundays. Hence, we could not see any of them, but there were many new additions like Australian Panda, Single White Dolphin, Seals, and Penguins, etc. We took a lot of photographs and had a great time in the zoo and came back in the afternoon. In the evening, we simply chilled and had a party in our hotel among our friends.

That 2nd week, our training continued until Friday. Rakesh and I were visiting River Rhine regularly in the evening, whenever we got some time. It was very near from our training office, as well as from the hotel. One day, we took a ride in the river Rhine on the cruise for about an hour and enjoyed it thoroughly. The bank of the river was full of restaurants with all types of food and drinks. It was the last Friday in Dusseldorf and we thought of going to the river side again, as the next day we were supposed to leave Dusseldorf. I and Rakesh first went near the Rheinturm Tower, having a restaurant at the top, which was situated just at the bank of the river. That place was developed like a park, with lush green grass and beautiful landscape. Then we came towards the restaurant side, right on the bank of Rhine River. We were sitting in a pub and there was heavy snow storm. We were sitting adjacent to a heater stand, but it was extremely cold and all restaurants got closed due to heavy snow storm. Incidentally, all restaurants were open type restaurants with temporary structures. We were inside that shed, but were very scared to see the snow storm, that too by the side of the river, which lasted for almost an hour. This was totally a new experience for me and also for Rakesh. In fact, on the same day, we had booked tickets of an entertainment show in a theatre, with dinner. That theatre hall was also almost at the bank of the river and was at one end. The entrance ticket for the show was of 56 Euros and full of entertainment for 2 hours, with music, dance, and acrobatics. The most attractive part was the acrobatics inside water. There was a very large wine glass shaped container, full of water, inside which a young lady did her acrobatics dance. That was very attractive and it was a lifetime experience for us.

The next morning, we were supposed to go to Berlin from Dusseldorf. Our hotel was right in front of the railway station. The next day, was a Saturday and we got up early and went to the station. It was heavily raining and our train was scheduled to start at 7:40 am. With a lot of difficulty, we boarded the train and started for Berlin. Our train was a superfast train and we commuted more than 500 km in 4 hours. The train was no less than an aeroplane. The maximum speed it attained some time was more than 300 km/hour. Sufficient amount of food and even alcoholic beverages were available on board, which was very surprising for us. We got a new experience and had some can beer inside the train. The sight was also beautiful while travelling in the train. Around noon, we reached Berlin. From the station we went to our hotel, which was located almost in the heart of the city. It was a 4-star hotel with beautiful rooms and the dinning place was huge.

We had a plan to stay at Berlin for 2 nights. So, the day we reached, Rakesh and I walked through the streets nearby our hotel, just after checking in. The whole area was covered with snow and ice and that sight was very beautiful even from our hotel room. We had organised a half a day, conducted tour of Berlin from 3 pm to 7 pm. A smart lady came with a bus as our guide and we started exactly at 3 pm. She was giving a continuous commentary all throughout our trip and was explaining everything very nicely. We knew that Berlin is a place with an eclectic mix of history, culture and gorgeous sights.

Our first visit was Brandenburg Gate, which was an old city gate, historically famous, and was rebuilt about 20 years back. Then we went to the Reichstag which had a beautiful glass dome and its basically the German Government office. After that, we went to the Berlin Cathedral, where the German architecture was the main attraction. Our next visit was to an UNESCO world heritage site i.e., Berlin's Museum Island.

Then we went to the biggest landmark, 'East side gallery'. This place is premised as an international memorial for freedom and the massive stretch of the 'Berlin Wall' with a stretch of 1316 meters. This wall was full of paintings and signs of unity of East and West Berlin. During our visit, the entire site was covered with snow and we were virtually walking on the snow. We then went to Hitler's Bunker in Berlin. It is truly a historical place as Adolf Hitler was one of the most influential figures in German history. He left an undeniable stamp on the capital of Germany. Though, it had historical importance, but I personally did not find that particular place to be very attractive for a tourist.

Our next and the last visit was another land mark of German history. The memorial of the murdered Jews of Europe also known as 'The Holocaust Memorial' is a memorial in Berlin for the Jewish victims. The Holocaust Memorial designed by architect Peter Eisenman and engineer Buro Happold, was something very different and unique. It consists of a 2711 concrete slabs or "stelae" arranged in a grid pattern on a sloping field. It was a place for prayer too and we sat there for some time and had a different feeling. By the time we visited all these places, it was evening and we came back to our hotel.

The next day was a Sunday and the whole day was available with us to visit other visiting paces in Berlin. We first decided to visit the 'Berlin Tower'. It was the tallest structure in Germany and third tallest tower in Europe. The height of the tower is 368 meters. It is a Radio and TV tower but open to tourists to have a view of the whole area of Berlin from the top. We had to stand in a long queue to go inside the tower. Finally, we got a chance to go to the deck area which was at a height of 203.78 meters and had the beautiful view of Berlin. It had a beautiful restaurant and bar at 207.53 meters. In fact, it was a revolving restaurant and by the time we finished our visit of the deck area, after standing in a long queue, I felt like having a mug of beer. To my good luck, the happy hour had just begun, but that was only for cocktails. Nevertheless, as the climate was cool and pleasant, I preferred a cocktail. The smart bar tender with his head shaved, offered different cocktails and I asked for a Manhattan cocktail. As it was the happy hour, I was offered 1 drink free with the one that I purchased. It was a thrilling experience, having a cocktail in a revolving restaurant in the Berlin tower. My friend Rakesh joined with me along with another friend Pinaki. We had a great time and others were grumbling with us, because of the delay. But we three spent some quality time in the revolving restaurant, with the cocktail.

We then had our lunch and went to the river area for a boat ride. It was along the Spree River and the boat travelled through bridges and canals. It was a lovely ride and a sightseeing trip. After finishing the boat ride, we went to the 'Mercedes Benz Gallery'. It was unique and one of its kind. In a multi-storied building, all types of cars were on display. On two revolving tables, the oldest model and the latest model of car were on display. It was very interesting to see many models of cars and it was almost an exhibition gallery. After spending more than an hour, we noticed that it was already evening. We could not fathom that the whole day was spent in a pleasant manner and it became evening so early. We then proceeded to our hotel, had dinner and slept after a hectic yet pleasant day.

The next day, we were supposed to go to Katowice in Poland. That trip was also by train. That was a Monday and a holiday for the plant in Poland. We boarded the train from Berlin at 10 am. There was a scheduled change of train in between, which we were unaware of. However, only while boarding, we came to know about it, that we have to change the train half way through. Of course, it is very unusual and it happened on that particular day due to some railway problem. The distance was about 470 km and the terrain was very different. We had to get down at Wroclaw, which was in Poland and it was announced that we have to change the train there. The distance from Wroclaw to Katowice was around 190 km.

The first stretch of journey from Berlin to Wroclaw was just great, as the train was a superfast and bigger train. As usual, all food articles and beverages including alcohol was available in the train. The view outside was just great, as there was a huge forest land and many lakes, which we could enjoy during our journey. The panoramic scene was unforgettable. We had food and drinks inside the train and were relaxing. We reached Wroclaw at around 1 pm and got down at the station. We were bit disappointed to see the station as we started comparing it with Berlin, which was much bigger and better railway station. However, we did not have any choice but to wait in the station to board the next train to Katowice. We boarded the next train around 2 pm. It was a lousy train and as told by the guard of the train, it was a slow-moving train. The buggies were cramped and not very clean. However, we had no option but to board the train and it started around 2:10 pm. We all started comparing the previous trains and travel and were bit disappointed. It tock us about 3hrs 30 minutes to reach Katowice from Wroclaw. The only silver lining was the panoramic scene outside. Everything including the fields, forest, trees and house roof were covered with white snow. The best part was, in the patches of white snow-covered fields anc forest, Red Deer were grazing and there was many countryside, hills and forests to be seen all throughout the journey. We were extremely excited to see such beautiful scenery outside and finally we reached Katowice at around 6 pm.

Katowice was a huge station and was quite clean and beautiful. Katowice railway station was totally different and was much better and modern as compared to Wroclaw. The best part was that, a young lady had come to receive us to the station near our buggy itself. She was in fact from the hotel that we had booked to stay in. She was very polite and nice and escorted us to the hotel. When we came out of the station, found that the whole area and roads were covered with snow. Adjacent to the station, there was a big market complex with shopping mall and also a money exchange counter. The young lady guide showed us everything from a distance and simply asked us to walk with her on ice covered road and with all luggage.

We were expecting a vehicle to be present and would have taken us to the hotel. But she made us walk and we reached the hotel within 10 minutes, which we never expected. But, then, though we had trolley bags and shoulder bags, while walking on the ice, it was very difficult. However, it was again a unique experience and we were much relaxed after reaching the hotel. In the reception counter, there was again another young lady and her behaviour was very nice. She allotted the rooms to us and we went to our respective rooms. Since we had travelled for quite a long time, we were absolutely tired. After seeing the room, I was extremely happy. It was very spacious and all amenities were available. I had a hot water bath and slept for an hour. By then my friends called me to have dinner. As the hotel had a beautiful bar with snacks, I did not venture to go out to have a full-fledged dinner and enjoyed the evening with heavy snacks and a glass of wine.

The next day, we had our training in a Steel Plant and we were told to be ready by 9 am. The chief coordinator of M/s SMS Siemag had flown from Dusseldorf to Katowice to coordinate, which we were unaware of. His presence made our life and training easier, as he was very much acquainted with the locals and plant people. He also spoke English very fluently. The bus came on Tuesday morning, which was the first day of training and we started for the plant. It was a bit far from our hotel and took us about an hour to reach the plant. It was a steel plant owned by M/s Arcelor Mittal. The authorities were very happy to know that we would be reaching the plant at around 10 am for the first day of the training.

The road that we commuted, was full of snow and ice and dozers were continuously cleaning the road to get rid of the accumulated snow. We reached the plant after about an hour instead of the estimated 40 minutes. We had a nice reception on our arrival inside the plant at their administrative building. Our coordinator from SMS Siemag along with some top administrative people of M/s Arcelor Mittal were present there. We had our safety orientation first and were provided with all safety related personal protective equipment. Then we were deputed at SMS-II, which was built by M/s SMS Siemag, Germany. We first had an introductory session and then visited the plant. As it is a cold country, there was an overhead covered path way to reach SMS-II, right from the administrative block. Such experience of going about a kilometre through such an overhead pathway was a first-time experience in my life.

Every evening we reached the hotel from the plant at around 6 pm and then we had our leisure time. On the 2nd day we explored some good Asian eating joints after discussing with our hotel guys. The people in the hotel were very cooperative and ready to help in all manner. We proceeded to the market area and found good restaurants owned by people from Bangladesh, Pakistan, and also India. Different varieties of beer were available in plenty and was cheaper as compared to Germany and we all were enjoying the food with drinks. The next evening, after coming from the plant, we wanted to spend a good time in the evening. Rakesh and I started exploring some good entertainment theatre, may be with pole dance, like Germany. Finally, we could locate two of them and enjoyed few evenings along with our other friends. We marked a very typical and distinct difference with regard to the attitude of people in Poland. The behaviour and hospitality of Polish people was very nice. They were very warm hearted and had a perpetual helping attitude. That was also prominently visible even inside plant during training.

As we could discover all possible nearby places in Katowice, we did not have any problem to enjoy. We also went a shopping mall, which was very huge as compared to the one in Germany, that we had seen in Dusseldorf. There was a distinct difference between the shopping mall in Katowice and Dusseldorf. It was the influence of American brands, which was felt in Poland. The garment brands like Gap and Banana Republic, were in place which was not there in Dusseldorf. Similarly, many other US brands of different products were also available in that shopping mall. We bought certain items to take to India, from that mall, which was the biggest mall in Katowice. The currency of Poland was Zloty which is a cheaper currency than Euro. As we had Euro with us, it was easily getting exchanged in the shop itself.

We continued the training every day as per our schedule, in the plant and many technical inputs were given to us which was very interesting and fruitful to commission our plant in Rourkela Steel Plant after coming back to India. But again, at the back of our mind, we were thinking of visiting some European country during the week end, which most of us had not visited earlier. We finally decided to go to Italy during the weekend. One of our young team members Bibhudutta took the initiative to book all air tickets and also booking of hotels, etc. With the available time, we planned the best possible options in Italy.

Bibhudutta planned for Rome, Venice, and all other good places in Italy. He booked the hotel and flight for us and we made him our chief coordinator. We gave him full authority including the money and he also became our treasurer. On a Friday after the morning session of training, in the afternoon all twelve of us started from our hotel and went to Krakow by road, as Katowice did not have any International Airport. From Krakow International airport we went straight to Rome by the airline 'Ryne Air'. It was a 2-hour flight and we reached Rome at around 5 pm Italy time. We had booked "Ibis hotel" and did not know the route from the airport. When we asked people outside the airport, nobody was able to explain to us the location of the hotel, even though we had a map. In fact, language was a big problem and we found that the people were not very cooperative, as compared to the people of Poland or even Germany. However, after waiting for about 45 minutes, one bus came which was going towards, Hotel Ibis. We boarded the bus and reached our hotel after one hour, as the hotel was very far from the airport. Finally, we were relaxed to get into the hotel and after having a hot water shower, we had dinner and slept, as we were very much tired.

The next morning, we got up early and went to the main station of Rome named 'Termini Train station' from where all city tour starts. It was 8 am when we started form our hotel and the bus took only 40 minutes in place of an hour to reach Termini station, as we had started early. It was a huge station and outside the station many tourist counters were available. We bought a whole day "Hoff on, Hoff off" bus for the local tour and started our journey at around 9:30 am.

After, going to Italy from Poland, where we were living sometimes even in sub-zero temperature, it was very warm for us in Rome with a temperature as high as 18 to 19 degrees Celsius. However, it was a very pleasant climate, thinking of the temperature in April in India. As we all know Rome has a rich history, we were very much anxious to see and cover as much place as possible in a day, as we had an open ticket.

We boarded the bus near Termini station and our first stop was the world-famous Colosseum, which is the symbol of Rome and a UNESCO world heritage. The Colosseum is the largest amphitheatre built during the Roman empire. It was inaugurated in 80 AD. Historically, it offered gladiator fights, execution, and animal hunts. Though some portions were broken, the gigantic look of the Colosseum was extraordinary and a feeling of old and rich heritage of human civilization came to my mind. It also reminded me of the Nalanda university of India, because of the look, though both were built for two different purposes. I was lucky to have visited Nalanda in 1993 with my parents. Nalanda University is also one of the UNESCO world heritage sites and one of the oldest universities in the world, which was built in 500 BC and continued until 700 AD. I had the pride of comparing our Indian civilisation with Roman civilisation, after seeing the Colosseum.

Then we proceeded to the Roman forum, located near the Colosseum. This was again a gigantic structure, which was the hub of political and social activities of the Roman citizens. In that place, religious and public affairs were going on in ancient days. Next, we went to Trevi Fountain, which is the most beautiful fountain in Rome. It is the largest fountain having 20 meters' width and 26 meters' height. The origin of this fountain goes back to the 19 BC, in which the fountain formed the end of the Aqua Virgo aqueduct. Our next trip was to Piazza Navona, which was a combination of 3 fountains surrounding mansions and was the most beautiful square in Rome. As decided earlier, we wanted to cover as many places as possible in a day.

Our next place of visit was the Vatican City, which is situated almost at the centre of Rome. Since I read and knew, it is the smallest country in the world and has its own history, thought to be situated in a secluded place. But to my surprise, it was very small and situated almost at the centre of Rome. The area is extremely beautiful with Roman architecture and St. Peter's square at the centre. It is one of the largest and beautiful squares in the world. It was designed by Bernini during 17th century. The most impressive parts of the square, beside the size are its 284 columns and 88 pillars that flank the square in a colonnade of 4 rows. Above the columns, there are 140 statues of saints, created in 1670. There are 2 fountains also in the centre which further enhanced the beauty of the place. The mind-boggling architecture of overall Rome, including the Vatican City, fascinated us to a great extent. We, in fact, skipped our lunch as we were engrossed in enjoying the whole city, given, we had only one day in hand and the next day we were supposed to go to Venice.

We had some snacks and bought a lot of souvenirs in Rome and by the time we came back to the hotel, it was 9 pm and we were extremely tired. We had a heavy dinner in a nearby restaurant and slept, as we had to get up early in the morning, the next day. We checked out from the hotel and went to the Termini Rail station for our journey to Venice by train. We boarded the train at around 8 am and reached Venice at around noon. It was a superfast train and as good as that of Germany. The view outside was just great and beautiful. After reaching Venice we boarded a shuttle, which straight took us to the hotel. It was also Ibis, but though smaller than Rome, was much spacious and beautiful. There was a big swimming pool with a beautiful garden in the hotel. After checking in, we sat by the side of the pool and enjoyed coffee.

In the afternoon, around 2 pm we started from the hotel to explore Venice. The climate was absolutely great and the roads were empty as compared to Rome. Knowing well that Venice is a city of immense beauty and historical significance, we set forth to explore it. We first went to the Grand Canal and saw the original Gandola and varieties of boats to travel in the river, crossing different canals. Since in "Gandola" manual rowing is involved, we chose to have a ride in motorised boat. The advantage of the motorised boat was that, six of us who were interested for a ride could be accommodated. It was an amazing experience to go through several houses and under small bridges for about an hour. In fact, Venice has literally hundreds of canals that connect various islands which make up the city and the largest of which is the Canale Grande. The monumental canal is more like a river and it passes from one side of Venice to the other and merges through the centre in a "S" bend shape.

As one of the bridges that spans the impressive Grand Canal, the Ponte di Rialto is undoubtedly the most famous and iconic sites through which we went in our boat. Originally a wooden bridge stood for hundreds of years until it collapsed in 1524. After that incident, an ornate stone bridge was built, that still stands today. We then went to St. Mark's Square which is the most famous square and a happening place in Venice. Opposite to the island of San Giorgio Maggiore this square holds huge importance in Venice and is a truly a spectacular place to visit. We could see many land mark buildings in the square including St Mark's Campanile, which is the tallest structure in Venice. There were many souvenir shops in that area and we bought quite a few of them for our family and friends.

We then went to the famous Lido Island, which creates a barrier between Venice and the Adriatic Sea and features a long stretch of beautiful beach to enjoy. It was a much calmer, laid back, and relaxed place as compared to central Venice. Lido island served as a true escape and provided stark contrast to the busy streets and water ways surrounding the Grand Canal. Since, by the time we reached the beach of Lido Island, it was dusk, we were extremely tired. There were beautiful open-air restaurants by the sea side, which served nice food and varieties of beer. Rakesh, I, and another friend Pinaki, sat on a table and had some beer, enjoying the sea breeze. We saw a huge cruise moving in the sea and we waved at the passengers from a distance and they waved back, which was a very fascinating experience. Our other friends were having fun in the sea water and later on, we three also joined them to bathe in the sea. After enjoying for more than an hour, we came back to our hotel and by then it was already 10 pm. Though the day was hectic, we had a great experience. Since on the next day, we had our return journey, we slept and got prepared for our return journey to Katowice, Poland.

The next day, we boarded the train at Venice and went first to Rome again. From the Termini railway station, we directly went to the airport. After a fantastic tour to Italy, it was a bit painful to return to Poland for the training. All throughout the journey from Venice till the hotel at Katowice, we were only discussing about our trip to Italy.

The next day, as usual we went for the training in the morning and met all the people, who were involved in training. As every day we were going inside the plant for our onsite training and not to any class room, it became easier for us to discuss the Italy trip. Since, our training was scheduled up to Friday, we had few days in hand to enjoy in Poland.

As we had not visited any place, other than Katowice in Poland, our training guide strongly recommended to visit the tourist spots of Krakow. On Thursday afternoon, after our training, we visited Krakow. It was snowing on that day and we were fully covered with winter clothes, jackets etc. But still the climate was windy and not suitable for tourism. As we did not have any option, in that condition, we travelled and visited Krakow. But the experience was something different and unforgettable.

First, we went to main market square, which was the largest medieval market in Poland, that was turned to a centre for social life of young students and people from all over the world. We did some shopping from there and went round the places, holding umbrella in our had, as it was drizzling. Our training guide also had accompanied us during the Krakow visit and hence it became easy to see the nice places in a short period of time and in such weather. We then went to the 'Wawel Royal Castle', which is one of the most important royal castles of Europe and the first UNESCO World Heritage site in the world. The castle had beautiful buildings, art galleries, churches, and defensive towers. It was the residence of most of the Polish rulers. The beauty of the castle was the land scape and the adjacent Vistula River. During our visit, the Vistula River looked completely white covered with snow. It was a unique sight for me, which I had never seen earlier in my life.

Adjacent to the castle and in between the castle and river Vistula, we visited the "Wawel Dragon" Statue, which is at the foot of the Wawel Hills in Krakow. It was a bronze statue designed by Polish sculpture Bronislaw Chromy. The statue has been described as a traditional element of modern Krakow landscape and a major tourist attraction of the city. The area was also covered with snow and the whole area was white, except the black bronze statue of the 'Dragon'. The memory of that site was so unique and beautiful that, it is still engraved in my mind.

As we knew, Krakow was famous for amber jewellery and it is called the "Amber city of Poland", it was worth visiting some good jewellery shop in Krakow. Our training guide also recommended strongly to visit the jewellery shop. Amber jewellery is one of the standouts of Polish contemporary design. After visiting different places, we went to a big jewellery shop. Basically, amber is made by craftsmen who handsomely shape the fossilised resin into unique and coveted pieces of jewellery. We found the shops selling reasonably priced souvenirs to costly designers neckless, bracelets, and rings. I could not resist taking a set for my wife which was yellowish brown in colour and also elegant. Though it was a bit costly, I bought that set. After having a beautiful and unique snowy day at Krakow, we came back to Katowice.

The next day was our last day of training inside the plant. We were given a warm farewell with certificate of successful completion of 2 weeks of training, which was very touching. I had taken some souvenirs and gave it to two of the training guides with whom I had developed very nice friendship. We then came to our hotel by 5 pm. As that was the last day and we were supposed to board the flight back to India, the next day, I thought of having some last-minute shopping from nearby shops. Then I and two more friends, wanted to visit the nearby market complex, adjacent to the railway station, of which we had a glance from a distance on the day of our arrival at Katowice in Poland. I did not visualize, that such a huge shopping mall was there along with all types of food counters in such a nearby place. Though, it was not as big as the shopping mall that we had visited on the second day of our stay at Katowise, but was very modern and beautiful. After a thorough round of the complex, I went to the money exchange counter to exchange the Polish Zloty to Euro. Then I and two of my friends, had food in Mc Donald's and came back to the hotel a bit early.

It was around 7 pm and we started packing our luggage, as on the next day we had our return flight to India from Krakow to Dubai via Frankfurt.

We had enjoyed Poland so much that it was very painful to leave the place and the country. The young lady, who was present in the reception counter, on our arrival, the same lady was present, before the day of our return journey. I thought of giving her a souvenir that I had taken from India, of my state of Odisha. I gave her a wall hanging called "Patta Chitra". She was overwhelmed and started weeping. Our whole group realised that the Polish people are different than other part of globe and are the most warm-hearted people that we had ever met anywhere in the globe.

I then became busy in packing my luggage and finished it within an hour and was ready by 9 pm. All the other friends were busy packing and running from one room to other, as they all had bought a lot of stuff and their luggage was overweight. Finally, our young friend Bibhudutta, who had organised the Italy trip, arranged one weighing spring to weigh each bag. But then, it was too late to discard any luggage and we all decided to carry the luggage as it is and pay the additional luggage charge.

 Finally, the next day which was a Saturday, the bus came and by 9 am we left the hotel and proceeded to the airport in Krakow. By 10:30 am, we reached the airport. It was the same airport from where we had flown to Rome, Italy. It took a bit of time in the airport for all the formalities. As predicted, except I and Rakesh, all the others paid extra luggage charge, and then we checked in. Incidentally, I and one friend named Prahalad checked in first and our luggage was booked directly to Indira Gandhi International Airport, New Delhi, India. The luggage of the rest of my friends, somehow, were booked only to Frankfurt, as there was a layover and even change of terminal and flight at Frankfurt.

We boarded the flight and reached Frankfurt at around 4 pm, which took around 2 hours. We landed in Terminal 1 and were supposed to go to Terminal 2, for our next flight to Dubai, which was scheduled to depart at around 10 pm by Emirates Airlines. Except Prahalad and I, all were supposed to collect their luggage from Terminal 1 and then go to Terminal 2. Since, I and Prahalad were not required collect the luggage, we immediately proceeded to Terminal 2. Frankfurt being one of the biggest and busiest airports, we wanted to have some time in hand. We went to Terminal 2 by a shuttle and before checking in, we enquired about our luggage status to be sure that, it will be delivered at Delhi in India. In a counter it was confirmed that our luggage is safe and we shall receive it in India. After getting the information from an authentic source, that our luggage is safe, we got relaxed and waited for other friends to arrive at the terminal. After arrival of remaining 10 members of our team, we proceeded, and checked in.

It was around six-and-a-half-hour journey from Frankfurt to Dubai and accordingly we reached Dubai at around 6:30 am (Dubai time). As usual, it was Air Emirates and we had a great time in the flight with regard to hospitality, food, and drinks. Our next connecting flight to Kolkata, India, was at 1pm in the afternoon and we had sufficient time in hand to hang around and shop from the duty-free shops. In fact, Dubai airport has 3 terminals and we arrived at Terminal-1. Our flight was scheduled to depart from Terminal-3. It is indeed a huge airport and posed difficulty for us in terms of covering the whole area. However, as we were acquainted with the airport during our onward journey, you could manage. As we reached in the morning and travelled throughout the night, the most important activity was to go to the wash room. Dubai being a huge airport and a transit place for many airlines, the morning was too crowded. After freshening up, we went to for shopping. We went in rotation, as the luggage was supposed to be taken care of. I and one of my friends went to a South

Indian joint and had Dosa. Having Dosa after more than a month, the taste was simply ethereal.

After having breakfast, we went for shopping. I was never interested to buy gold and was interested to buy chocolates and alcohol. I bought a bottle of 'Remy Martin VSOP' cognac, a bottle of 'Johnnie Walker, Explorer's Club' whiskey, and varieties of chocolates. I also bought some good perfume for my family members. That was enough for me and I spent only around 45 minutes to 1 hour for shopping as I was very clear as to what I am required to buy. Since our flight was at 1 pm and from Terminal-3, we proceeded to the terminal around 11 am and reached there within 15 minutes. We still had sufficient time in hand and the friends who had plans to further shop could do it in Terminal-3. We boarded an Air Emirates flight from Dubai and reached Kolkata at around 6 pm. It was obviously a nostalgic feeling to reach the home land. But at the same time, we had a long way to go, considering we had to pass the immigration, customs, and above all, again we would have to travel by train to our place Rourkela. That evening, from Kolkata airport, we went straight to Hotel Peerless at Kolkata. We stayed overnight, as our train was scheduled on the next day at 1 pm. We had a great time that evening, as we organised a party in the hotel, since that was the last day of our union. The next day we boarded the train at 1 pm and reached Rourkela at around 7:30 pm.

Chapter 10:

2013- An Eventful Year

It was a great feeling reaching home after visiting Europe and that too, for more than a month. After my arrival at Rourkela, Rachita and my parents were very happy, as well as excited to see me after such a long time. However, at that time my father was not keeping too well as he was 86 years old. Rachita had taken care of my father, in addition to her day job and that too when I was away for a long time. There was a lot of admiration for Rachita on the part of my parents. I had brought several gifts for my friends and family and had taken thousands of photographs. So, we spent the next 2 days seeing those photographs and the gifts.

Thereafter, I started attending my plant duty. I was transferred from Steel Melting Shop-II to Steel Melting Shop-I by that time. Hence, I joined SMS-I as Head of Mechanical Section. Initially I was a bit disappointed, as I was trained for the upcoming Slab Caster-3 of SMS-II, but transferred to SMS-I. However, I decided to take things as they came. In SMS-I, I had more time available than SMS-II and also, I was well acquainted to SMS-I, as I had a long tenure earlier. Thereafter, I started reading different journals on Steel making, Secondary Metallurgy, and as such I was trained on Continuous casting. I also read books on metallurgy and took keen interest in Steel making. During those time, I also got the opportunity in several occasions to work as Head of Department. In that position, it was more necessary to know about the production, rather than maintenance. My reading and writing habit, gave me an edge over other maintenance friends, with regard to steel making. That also helped in making better quality of steel and eventually the productivity also increased.

The same year 2013, had been a very eventful year for us. Anisha, after passing out from TISS in 2008 and joined the CSR of a corporate in Mumbai, through campus interview. She worked for about one and half years and quit the job to work in a hard-core NGO again in Mumbai, who were working for women empowerment. She enjoyed her new role and preferred to work in the field. She started writing articles on women empowerment in different magazines and journals. She even conducted road shows, depicting women empowerment. The interesting part is, her salary got reduced in the new assignment, but still she preferred to continue. In the meantime, she was preparing for MPhil in the University of Cambridge, without letting us know about it. She also cleared some examination and scored good marks for joining in Cambridge. In the final stage of selection, she revealed that she is going for advance study to Cambridge. She also said, that joining the hard-core NGO, in spite of getting less salary, was one of the reasons for her future endeavour to join the University of Cambridge. That was truly a pleasant surprise for all of us.

She went to Cambridge in August 2011 and did her MPhil and came back to India in September 2012 after successfully completing her course. After coming back from Cambridge, she joined in a company on education and training. She was enjoying her new company and the new role. It is during that time she was prepared to get married to her boyfriend Anil, in the month of May/June '2013. That very year i.e., 2013, my father fell seriously ill and passed away in June. As per normal ritual, we could not conduct the marriage of our daughter immediately at our place Rourkela and it was a destination wedding in the month of November at Bangalore. A club named 'Bowring Club' was booked for our stay. In the same venue cocktail, sangeet, etc., was also conducted. As, it was a destination wedding for us, my daughter and son-in-law organised everything for the marriage and we were only the facilitating resources. I invited my close friends and relatives for the wedding. Around thirty of us, went from Rourkela to Bangalore by train. We had a great time, right from the train journey till the end of the wedding. My daughter's friends also came from all around the globe as she also studied in the University of Cambridge, UK, apart from TISS in Mumbai. Eventually, for Anisha's friends who came from different parts of the globe like USA, UK, Singapore, South Africa etc, Bangalore became an easier and better destination to come, due to much better connectivity. On the day of wedding, all the friends of Anisha were wearing sarees and had put on mehndi on their palms, which was giving a beautiful look and feeling. Although there were not many guests, the whole marriage ceremony went quite well and everybody were extremely happy. After the wedding, Anisha changed her job and subsequently, joined a UK-based, Global Leadership Development organization.

My younger daughter Anooja also had completed her 5 years Integrated Law from Ram Manohar Lohia National Law University (RMLNU), Lucknow, with flying colours, in the same year 2013. As, she had done her specialisation in Intellectual Property Rights (IPR), she preferred to join an IPR firm and joined at Gurugram in Delhi-NCR and subsequently she changed her job to another IPR firm in same Gurugram and is continuing there.

In the year 2013, the demise of my father, the marriage of Anisha, graduation of Anooja in Law and joining her new job, to start her professional career, all happened within the same year. By then I and my wife were a bit tired. One evening in the month of January 2014, Rachita and I were discussing in the evening about some outing to a good foreign destination/holiday resort to relax. But the planning was done for 2015, as we did not want to go anywhere before the completion of 1st death anniversary of my father, until June 2014. Rachita, was always interested to go to Europe and I was interested to go to USA again. Finally, after several discussions, we planned to visit several parts of Europe and also USA. Making a plan was very exciting and we made the plan for our visit in May/June 2015, which was for more than a month. Fortunately, M/s Cox and Kings office was already established at Rourkela with very positive feedback from many people. Hence, it became easier for us to plan our trip in a better way. Probably, given a chance, my wife would have travelled all over Europe for a month, including the country side, but not USA. However, seeing my interest for USA, she again discussed with me. We had a detailed discussion with the M/s Cox and Kings and made a tailor-made programme, which they called 'Flexi Holidays'. In my mind, I had decided that, it would be the last visit to Europe and USA, before my superannuation in May'2018.

Another important aspect also had come to our mind, as we were supposed to conduct our younger daughter Anooja's marriage at Rourkela, which most of our friends and relatives had requested for. Further, we had decided the wedding to be conducted before my superannuation in 2018. Hence, we thought to have the best of our tour to my capability, before the wedding of Anooja. Accordingly, we started planning the tour of Europe and USA.

Interestingly, as I was always in touch with my Maternal uncle in USA, with whom we stayed for a week during the 2007 visit. Hence, I discussed our tentative itinerary with him as he was a great traveller and I said that we would positively visit the UK, starting from the city of London. Accordingly, I took his advice and chose to go to London via Vienna, Austria, which I had never visited in the past. But this time we did not stay with my maternal uncle, as he was away to his daughter's place at Seattle. I also called up my co-brother-in-law, Manoj about the USA visit. He proposed me to reach to his place by the first week of June, when he would be free and can give us sufficient time. As we were visiting London, we also spoke to one of our nephews named Chickoo, who was living in London. I thought it prudent to discuss with Chickoo about the visiting places in and around London, and asked him to let us know about some decent hotel or Bed & Breakfast arrangement in London. But he was so nice that he requested us to stay with him and did not allow us to stay in any hotel. We finally agreed to his proposal. As our daughter Anisha had studied in the University of Cambridge, we had a great desire to visit Cambridge also and our planning was done accordingly, after discussing with both Chickoo and Anisha.

Since, it was a plan of more than a month tour, it could be made possible only during summer holidays, when the school is closed for my wife. Hence, our planning was done from 2nd week of May to 3rd week of June 2015. As per the procedure, we were supposed to make the Schengen Visa and the UK visa at least 3 months earlier to the date of departure and we did not have any problem about USA visa, as the USA visa was valid up to May 2016. So, it was in the month of February, 2015, that we got an appointment for the UK visa, where it was necessary to go for a biometric and hence it was required to be present in person in the visa office. Once the UK visa was done, Schengen visa could be done easily, only through application and physical presence was not required at the visa office.

We proceeded to Kolkata in the month of February and went to the Kolkata office of M/s Cox and Kings. They gave us all the relevant documents and then we went to the UK visa office, which is in the south of Kolkata. Our appointment time was 11:45 am. We were on time and passed through all the papers. First my bio-metric was done and I was cleared. I was extremely happy that I would get my visa positively. But, during the bio-metric of my wife, there was an error and finally it was detected that, in the first page, in the field of 'Sex', it was printed 'M' in place of 'F', which is Male in place of Female. It was a big shock to us and the only alternative was to make a fresh passport. We were totally upset and came back to Rourkela the same evening by train. The next morning, we reached Rourkela and my wife went to

Bhubaneswar by bus, as the issuing passport office was in Bhubaneswar. With a lot of effort, we received her new corrected passport. Fortunately, we had adequate time and again we took appointment for the bio-metric for UK visa. In the meantime, I received my visa, but had to rush again to Kolkata for my wife. Since all other papers were cleared, there was not much of hassle for the biometric and we came back the same evening to Rourkela. There was a total delay of 15 days, with respect to the receipt of my visa and her visa. We were so relaxed after getting her visa, that it cannot be expressed in words.

Chapter 11:

Whisky, Waterfalls, and Wanderings in Europe

After getting the visa with lot of difficulties by the end of February'2015, we finally started our preparation of our tour. We started from Rourkela to Bhubaneswar on the 14th of May, 2015, by train, stayed there for a day, and the next day flew to Delhi. Our younger daughter, Anooja was living in Gurgoan at that time. She was staying with her friends in a flat nearby the flat of our nephew Saurav. We used to stay with Saurav at Gurugram, every time, that we went to Delhi. It was this time also where we stayed and did our last-minute purchases for more than a month-long trip to Europe and the USA.

Our flight was scheduled on the 17th night (18th morning, 1:30 am) by Austrian Airlines via Vienna to London. We took a layover in Vienna so that we can take a half-day conducted tour of Vienna and could board the flight in the evening for London. We boarded the flight from Terminal-3 at Delhi International Airport at 1:30 am. It was a beautiful flight with delicious food and beverages. At the same time, the crew members were very nice. Rachita, slept immediately on the flight and I followed after taking a glass of wine, as the next day we were supposed to have a whole day tour of Vienna.

It was around 8 hours' flight and we reached Vienna at about 6 am (Vienna time). The airport was small as compared to London, Paris, Switzerland, etc., by European standards. But it was extremely beautiful and clean. We, went to the lounge after all formalities, as we had the Priority Pass. We had a nice breakfast and were ready for the tour. We had booked our luggage directly to London and Rachita was carrying only a handbag. Our conducted tour was scheduled from 9:30 am to 2 pm. We had a booking in a super-fast metro rail and we reached our starting point of the tour around 8:30 am. We were the first couple to reach the spot and subsequently, many tourists assembled and our bus started exactly at 9:30 am, with a very nice lady guide. It was amazing to see the city and the different tourist spots.

We had chosen a tour which showed us both modern and historic highlights. First, we drove around the ring of Vienna's most famous boulevard and we had the 'Skip the line' type tickets for everywhere. First, we went to Schonberg Palace, which was a colossal 1441 room structure. It was designed in baroque style with impeccable symmetry and had different statues on the rooftop. Inside, the palace was fully furnished and decorated in the original style, and there were paintings which were so lively that they almost looked 3D. Next, we went to Hofburg Palace. This palace is another huge palatial complex that was nothing but a tribute to the power and influence of the Habsburg dynasty. It was also the main winter palace for the rulers of the Austro-Hungarian Empire for hundreds of years. But during our visit, it was already converted to the office of the President of Austria. This building was constructed in the 13th century and we could appreciate the baroque architecture. In that place, the garden with the fountain was very beautiful and we met one young lady from Russia, who was perusing masters in "History". She also discussed our Indian history with us and, said that her future visit would be to India. She also took a photograph with us.

Then we proceeded to the St. Stephen's Cathedral. It was an iconic building, being the tallest church not only in Vienna but also in Austria. The Romanesque and Gothic design of the exterior, to the dominating pointed tower and the intricately decorated main roof complete with hundreds of coloured tiles forming an intriguing pattern, was extremely beautiful, and worth watching. We then proceeded to Rathaus, which was again the Town hall, that was built in the 18th century and was constructed in the Neo-Gothic style. After having spent some time there, we finally went to Schonbrunn's garden. Our last visit was the garden, where we could spend some time there and relax. The garden was more than a kilometre long, the flowers were in full bloom and it was very beautiful. After visiting the garden, we were tired and hungry. We could see a pool and a classical colonnaded long building, where we found the cafe. We enjoyed our food and drink there and relaxed for some time.

By then it was the time for our return journey. We boarded the bus around 2 pm and reached the railway station within 10 minutes. We had our return ticket in the first class of that superfast train and reached the airport at around 3 pm. We again went to the lounge to freshen up, after a hectic day. Our flight to London was scheduled for 5:30 pm. We relaxed for a while and finally boarded the flight and reached London at 8 pm. We had to wait for our luggage and finished our immigration formalities. We were in touch with our nephew Chickoo. When we came out of Heathrow airport, we saw him waiting there for us. It was such a nostalgic moment for both of us. Rachita had met him earlier, and our daughter Anisha, while studying in University of Cambridge had also stayed with them. I met him for the first time and found him to be very warm. We went to his house by his car and reached within half an hour. We had taken lots of gifts for his wife and the 3-year-old son. After receiving a warm welcome at their house in Reading, we had our dinner. Next day, since we had a special open ticket for the day for our tour, we got up leisurely and took all the tips from Chickoo on the breakfast table.

Chickoo was supposed to go to the office and he dropped us at the nearest metro station. We went near Piccadilly Circus, which took 30 minutes, and then we decided to board a 'Hop on Hop off' bus and went around all the places without getting down anywhere. Then as per our choice and bookings, we got down at Madam Tussauds Wax Museum. We were surprised to see the queue and thought, it would not be possible to get inside before a minimum of 2 hours. I went and showed our ticket to an official and he explained that ours was a special ticket called "Skip the line" type and we need not stand in the queue. We then went inside the wax museum. This museum was much bigger and better, as compared to the one I had seen in 1996 in Amsterdam. Rachita and I enjoyed a lot in the museum. We took photographs with the wax statue of celebrities like Amitabh Bachchan, Shahrukh Khan, Madhuri Dixit, George Clooney, and many more.

Inside the museum, we also found a small toy train, which was moving in a zig-zag manner from top to bottom, for which one has to buy a separate ticket, which was optional. However, for us, it was included in our special ticket and we had the privilege to go for a ride. We discovered that they had devised the toy train for a unique reason. The ride was called "Sprit of London taxi ride" and we could see several incidents and events of London having some historical importance like London fire, Plague etc. and finally how they have overcome all those and having different joyful celebrations at London, which was depicted through wax statues. The toy train ride inside the museum was with a light and sound arrangement and was very enjoyable. The overall experience in the 'Madam Tussauds' museum was just great.

We then went to a money exchange counter to exchange some Euros to Pound and then proceeded to 'Piccadilly Circus' which was a road junction and public space in Westminster. It was a truly happening marketplace. We spent some time and then went to the Buckingham Palace. Since that was the first visit for my wife, we spent sufficient time in all the landmark visiting places. We enjoyed the sight and the total surrounding of the palace. The guards of the palace were mounted on horses, carrying guns, looked smart. We then sat in the garden in front of the palace and relaxed for some time and also compared the visit to our Mysore palace in India. As we felt hungry by that time, we thought of having lunch and went to a beautiful restaurant and had the famous 'Fish and Chips'. Our next visiting place was 'Trafalgar Square'. It is one of the most important public squares in the city of Westminster, Central London. The typical architecture and the fountain at the centre were very beautiful. To add to the attraction, thousands of affable pigeons were dabbling around in that place.

We visited so many places that we did not realize, it was already evening and proceeded back to Reading with some gifts for Chickoo's son. We then had dinner with their family and at the dining table we discussed the next day's programme. As we wanted to visit Cambridge, the next day, Chickoo guided us on how to go there. The main purpose to visit Cambridge was that Anisha studied at the 'University of Cambridge' and was always appreciating not only the kind of education that she received there but also how beautiful the place was. The next morning, we went to 'Kings Cross Railway Junction' from where we had to board the train for Cambridge. We had a voucher for the train and initially thought that to be the ticket. Fortunately, we asked at the help desk and they explained to us that we have to get a ticket from the counter or retrieve the ticket from a computerized kiosk with the help of the voucher. The queue at the counter was too long and hence we preferred to go to the kiosk. One gentleman helped us, and we got the tickets in no time. We then immediately rushed and boarded the train. The journey was just great and it was a super-fast train. The view outside was beautiful and we reached Cambridge within an hour.

Cambridge was a small station but was very beautiful. When we came out of the station, we felt a sense of familiarity, though that was our first visit, we had listened so much about the place and the university.

We then boarded a bus and went near the university. It was such a lovely place with so many colleges, walking around the streets was an amazing experience. We preferred to first visit Trinity College and King's College. The architecture and the buildings were majestic. We met some professors and took photographs with them. We also saw, most of the people are riding bi-cycle there. Then, we went for a punting in the River Cam, as strongly recommended by Anisha. It was a manual boat ride in the river alongside all the colleges at the University of Cambridge. The ride lasted for more than an hour and interestingly, the boatman was a student in the university. The lush green lawn, gardens, and creepers were seen all along, with ducks roaming in many places. Even some buildings were so full of creepers that the wall was not visible. It was an amazing and unique experience to go for a punting and see the majestic view.

By then, we felt like having food and had our lunch in a beautiful restaurant, which Anisha had recommended. After lunch, again we went around several colleges, including Girton College where Anisha was studying, to have a feel of her college. It was mind boggling to see such college ambience and the overall Cambridge University. We did not have a plan for an overnight stay and by evening, we boarded the train and came back to London. From London, we proceeded to Reading to Chickoo's place. We described the whole day's experience at the dining table, while having dinner and all enjoyed our narration. We also discussed the next day's plan for the London visit, as that would be our last day in London.

The next morning, we again went to Trafalgar square, which both of us loved, and then walked down to the bank of River Thames. We went for the boat ride and had a beautiful experience crossing several bridges and seeing Big Ben. The narration of the guide was just great, as she explained every iconic landmark throughout the ride. She also explained about the London Eye. Our next plan was in fact, to have the ride in the London Eye which interestingly was built a couple of years after my debut visit to London in London in 1996.

London Eye is situated just on the bank of River Thames and it's a gigantic wheel which was inaugurated on the 31st of December'1999. We went there and were not required to stand in the queue, as our entry ticket issued by M/s Cox and Kings was having a special status, same as the "Madam Tussauds" museum. We were very excited to have a ride in the wheel. London Eye was also called Millennium Wheel and is a cantilevered observation wheel. It's Europe's tallest cantilever wheel and the most popular tourist attraction. The diameter of the wheel is 120 meters and the total height is 135 meters. For completing one revolution it took about 30 minutes. It has 32 air-conditioned capsules with full safety. However, the numbering was from capsule 1 to 33, as number 13 was not allotted to any capsule. We virtually laughed at the numbering system, as the British people always call us as superstitious, but instead they are more superstitious. Particularly, when we saw that number "13" has not been allotted to any capsule of, one of the most iconic landmarks 'The London Eye' in the centre of London, it was very surprising for us.

We sat in capsule 9 and it started moving. Sitting on such a wheel was a lifetime experience and moving at such a slow speed was also very unique. The view of the River Thames, different buildings, and the whole of London with a beautiful blue sky line, was just great. It was such an amazing experience that it cannot be explained in words. After the ride, we did not feel like doing anything or visiting any place, though we had an open ticket for 3 days London visit. I felt like sitting in a cosy place and having a draught beer with fish and chips. We walked and crossed the bridge and sat outside a restaurant. We spent about 2 hours outside the restaurant and there we relaxed and discussed the overall experience of the London visit. It was simply mindboggling to discuss the beautiful experience, as we were supposed to leave London, the next day, and move to Scotland.

We started for Reading and reached around 7:30 pm at Chickoo's place. The next day, 9:30 am was the scheduled time of our train for Edinburg from King's Cross station. Since we had our onward journey from Scotland, we packed all our luggage and started early in the morning. We reached King's Cross station and boarded the train, as it was departing from King's Cross only. We had our ticket in the 1st class and it was again a superfast train. We chose to travel to Edinburg by train to see the beauty of the landscape, forest, etc., in that 4-hour journey. The train had a beautiful pantry car and few lady hawkers were also moving inside the train. Food, snacks, and both alcoholic and non-alcoholic beverages were available on the train. We had burgers, chips etc. in the train. Finally, I wanted enjoy a beer, as the journey was bit long and the land scape outside was extremely beautiful. We both thoroughly enjoyed the train journey from King's cross, London to Edinburg.

We reached Edinburgh at around 2 pm and the driver of our vehicle was waiting for us with a plaque card. We had our hotel booking in 'Old Waverley', which was situated in Princes' Street. The driver suggested, we walk with him instead of boarding the taxi and he picked up all our luggage. We simply followed him and reached our hotel within 10 minutes. He finally explained that the car would have taken more than 30 minutes and hence he suggested walking to the hotel. We also enjoyed the walk with him, as the breeze was nice, and sitting on the train for more than 4 hours, was a bit claustrophobic too.

We checked in and relaxed for some time. Around 6 pm we walked through the streets. Our hotel was situated in the main road central market area. The people of Scotland were very nice and always would smile at us. The place was a bit laid back and the people were very warm. After walking for an hour in that vicinity, we searched for an

Indian restaurant and got it. We had a nice early dinner and then came back to our hotel, as that was the first day of our stay in Edinburgh.

The next morning, we were having the city tour by the 'Hop on Hop off' bus. Incidentally, the stop was just adjacent to our hotel. We had an awesome hot breakfast with varieties of spreads. By 9:30 am we were at the bus stop. We had already decided the places to visit and accordingly, first we went to the world-famous and most iconic landmark- Edinburg Castle. This castle had a historic importance, which dominates the skyline of Edinburg, the capital city of Scotland. When we reached near the castle and saw the view from a distance, I could not resist and we got down from the bus and preferred to walk uphill. I took several photographs from different angles with my camera and slowly walked to the castle. At the entrance, a man was playing a Bagpiper with the typical dress of Scotland. The man was wearing a 'Kilt' the knee-length skirt-like garment, which is typically the national grab of Scotland. Rachita and I took photographs with the man. It was an amazing experience to see such a sight and then we walked further. Finally, we reached the big flat surface and relaxed there for some time. There were some official guides, who were explaining the history of the castle, free of cost. The best sight was the 2 big cannon and even during our visit, it was in working condition. Every day at 1 pm, except Sunday, the cannon is fired and it is a spectacular sight. The bore of the cannon was 20 inches and was maintained in perfect condition, though it was built in the year 1449. Unfortunately, the day we visited, it was a Sunday, and we could not see the cannon being fired.

It was almost afternoon, and then we went to the Holyrood Palace. It is the official residence of the British monarch in Scotland. It was located at the opposite end of Edinburg Castle. This palace served as the principal residence of the Kings and queens of Scots since the 16th century. Queen Elizabeth spends one week in that palace at the beginning of every summer.

After the visit to the Holyrood Palace, we had our lunch and then visited the National Museum of Scotland. It was such a huge museum that it would take more than a day to see the museum properly. Still, we thought of spending 2 to 3 hours, as it was very fascinating. It was a museum having a collection covering science and technology, natural history, world culture etc. It also has a rich collection of Scottish antiquities, culture, and history. We visited all five floors, but most fascinating in the museum was the 'Tyrannosaurus Rex', which is nothing but the fossil of a Dinosaur and the length is 12 meters with a 6 meters' tail. The next attraction was the rooftop terrace of the National Museum, from where we could see the panoramic view of Edinburg and the old town, in particular, was just great.

 Our next visit was the 'Millennium Garden'. This lovely garden with its French-style parterre was created to commemorate the new millennium and features the intertwining initials of the 10th Duke and Duchess of Roxburghe. There was another plantation adjacent to the Millennium Garden, named 'Star Plantation'. This woodland garden was a man-made dense forest with a proper pathway to walk on. It was a nice experience walking through those plantations and enjoying the lush green man-made forest. Leisurely enjoying those beautiful gardens, we realised much later that it was already 6.30 pm.

By that time, we were tired and decided to go back to the hotel. We ordered some food from the adjacent Mc Donald's as takeaway and ate comfortably in our hotel. Our next day trip was 'Whisky and Waterfall' which I had deliberately chosen to not only see the forest, landscapes but to visit a distillery to know how whisky is made in Scotland and what makes it different from the rest. Rachita had a different interest in that tour to go a faraway place from the busy

Edinburgh city and enjoy the countryside, forest, and mountain cliff, etc.

The next morning, we had to go quite early to the starting point of our tour, which was a bit far from our hotel. We hired a cab and reached the tourist office at 8:30 am. It was a Mercedes minibus and the driver was the guide of our tour. He was wearing the typical traditional dress of Scotland Kilt. Exactly at 9 am, we started from Edinburg and we were the only Indian couple on that tour. The mini-bus travelled through a beautiful forest, full of lush green landscape and snow cliff mountains. The scenery was out of the world. Rachita was extremely thrilled and she started comparing it with our previous journey from Luzern to Interlaken in Switzerland. That journey was by train in the 'Golden pass' route in 2007. But then, she was extremely happy with this tour by bus in the countryside and the beautiful terrain of Scotland and was saying, it was better than Switzerland. She was recapitulating, what she had read in some books about Scotland and her thrill was doubled.

The wind through the Scottish Highland and the sight of the majestic mountains near the Turret River was surreal. On the way to the highland, we stopped at the base of the mountain, where there was a 30 minutes' break. It was situated just at the foot of the mountain and the scenic beauty was fantastic. It was very breezy in that place and we enjoyed hot coffee in a kiosk. Two of our co-passengers went towards the mountain and forgot that there was only a 30 minutes' break. We all waited for about 45 minutes for them. That couple was from Turkey and were very young. We then proceeded towards the Glen Turret distillery which was tucked away in a beautiful green valley, surrounded by nothing but the sounds of nature. On the way, we enjoyed several mountains covered with snow and beautiful lakes, and finally reached the Glen Turret distillery. The distillery was situated outside the picturesque village of Crieff in Perthshire.

It was the oldest distillery in Scotland. The very entrance had an antique look and the interiors were awesome. The tour name was 'The Famous Grouse experience'. One guide having a beard, started explaining the making of Single malt whisky and told us the difference between Single malt and Blended whisky. I could understand the full making of whisky and the importance of Casks and how long it is required to be matured. After having explained about the whisky-making, we went to one of the greatest attractions, which was a blended whisky bottle of 'The Famous Grouse', the one which had received the Guinness World Record. The height of the bottle was 5feet 7inches and it had 228 litres of whisky. Rachita and I got amazed and took several photographs with the bottle, which was fascinating and altogether a different experience. Then, we were taken to the warehouse where the casks full of whisky were kept. Finally, at the exit, there was a beautiful bar and sales counter where we were offered 2 varieties of whisky for a free tasting and were served with 2 small pegs of 30 ml of different varieties of whisky. I had the pleasure of tasting and having the small pegs of whisky. With such a cold atmosphere with the cold breeze, it worked well for me. By then we were feeling hungry. Adjacent to the distillery, there was a beautiful restaurant where we had lunch followed by coffee.

After a break of about 1 hour, we again started our journey and went near a jungle and walked through it for about more than a kilometre. We were proceeding to a natural beauty spot with incredible waterfalls. While walking through, after about 500mts, we discovered around 50 men, women, and children draped in beautiful dresses, were enjoying in the deep jungle. We saw them carrying and keeping several cane baskets with wine and full of flowers. Our Scottish guide asked us not to disturb them and explained that a 'Destination wedding' was being celebrated. It was a very unique experience for us. After seeing such a beautiful sight, we further proceeded and could reach the spot where we could see several waterfalls. We cannot forget the spectacular sight of the waterfalls having spent more than an hour there. It was almost 7 pm that we started on our return journey after such a lovely tour named 'Whisky and Waterfall'. While narrating the whole day's experience and writing, I am getting goose bumps.

At around 9.30 pm, we reached our hotel and relaxed that night. The next day was our scheduled flight to Paris. The flight was scheduled at 9 am from Edinburgh International Airport to Paris via Copenhagen. While checking out from the hotel, I asked the gentleman at the counter to talk to our travel agent M/s Cox and Kings to ensure a car as per the itinerary at De Gaulle International Airport, Paris. Accordingly, a reminder was given to the travel agent. By then, our pick-up car arrived and we proceeded for the airport. In that process, I forgot the room key to be delivered to the front desk counter. However, I realized that after checking in at the airport about the room key. I gave a call to the hotel about it, as 25 pounds was kept as security money through my credit card at the hotel. That money would not be returned to me unless I return the room key. At that point of time, I did not have any option but to fly to Copenhagen. There were 4 hours' layover at Copenhagen airport and we deliberately did not go out due to paucity of time and as such, our destination was Paris. The Copenhagen airport was not very big, but very beautiful and clean. After spending a couple of hours in the airport with good food and beverages, we boarded the flight to Paris and the flight duration was around 2 hours. We reached Paris at around 2 pm.

We came out from Charles De Gaulle airport and looked for our cab. I found one gentleman standing with the placard having the name 'Prabodh Ranjan Padhee'. I was very happy to see him and by then Rachita saw another gentleman standing with a placard having the name 'P R Padhee'. Both the persons claimed to be the driver assigned by Cox and Kings to pick us up, and both had the same flight details.

There was a big confusion for us and we were in dilemma, with whom to proceed to the hotel. In that process, we had lost around 45 minutes. Finally, I decided to call the international helpline number of Cox and Kings and could find out that, because I asked the reception in the hotel at Edinburgh in Scotland and told that my name was 'P R Padhee', the second vehicle was sent, otherwise, originally as per my itinerary the vehicle was there in the airport, in the name of 'Prabodh Ranjan Padhee'. When, we recapitulate that particular moment, it gives us a mixed feeling of fear and enjoyment. It was fearful because we had landed in a foreign soil and two people were claiming to be the driver and by then, several passengers and even cab operators had encircled us. It went to such an extent that one cab owner even said, they are frauds and he would drop us at our hotel. But at the nick of the moment, it struck to my mind to call up the international help line number of Cox and Kings, which saved us from uncertainty and anxiety and finally we boarded the right cab to reach our hotel.

I apologised to M/s Cox and Kings and rather appreciated their hospitality and response towards a call by the valued customer. Though there was a bit of delay, we were relaxed and proceeded to the hotel. Our hotel was near Champs Elysees and it took us around one hour to reach there. On the way, we were discussing about the Eiffel tower, as we had seen on TV that because of multiple cases of pickpocketing, the Eiffel tower had been closed. Our cab driver explained, that on the same day, it had been opened after 3 days. We were in seventh heaven, after knowing that the Eiffel tower has been opened on the day of our arrival.

We reached our hotel and were given a room on the 8th floor. It was a fantastic hotel with regard to cleanness, hospitality, and location in particular. We had lunch after reaching and took a rest in the hotel. We had the programme to go for 'Lido' show, for which we had pre-booked ticket arranged by M/s Cox and Kings. In 1996, when I visited

Paris, we did not have sufficient time and hence, were not able to see the show. It was always my desire to see the world-famous Lido in Paris and I was very excited that this time I got the opportunity to see the show. We had taken the ticket for the 7:30 pm show and as per the instruction on the voucher, we were supposed to reach there by 7 pm. We found from our travel desk that it was very near to our hotel and would take around 20 minutes to walk. However, since it was our first day, we did not take a risk and asked for a cab. Within seven minutes, we reached the place.

We had to stand in the queue for some time and we found many newlywed couples from all over the globe, who were standing in the queue. As per the dress code, we were wearing nice formal dress and similarly, all were well-dressed. We went inside the massive hall and found that the hall is a semi-circle and the stage is at the centre. The show started exactly at 7:30 pm. It was mesmerising to see the sparkling lights and the glittering feathers. The show was sensual, elegant, and spectacular, which took our breath away. There were talented artists, fascinating acrobats, incredible ice skaters, and glamourous elegant dancers. The Champs Elysees glorifies Parisian art and architecture and the capital city comes alive in the world's most beautiful avenue. The centre stage and the whole gallery had a telescopic arrangement. We were automatically going up and down, sitting in our own place, while watching the show, as the centre stage of the performing artists having the telescopic arrangement was also moving up and down. We realised that aspect a bit later, as it was happening rhythmically and accordingly, the whole semicircle stage was moving up and down. That part was something amazing. The 3-course dinner with red and white wine was just very exotic. We had a fantastic time and were out of the world for more than 2 hours inside the hall in the Lido. All the spectators like us, in the show were not allowed to take their own camera and take photographs during the show. The official photographers were taking photographs continuously and offered us to buy our photographs. We chose one and bought one. The very first-day experience in Paris was extremely great.

While returning after the show, we decided to walk, as we had gotten acquainted with the road to our hotel while coming for the 'Lido' show by the cab. Our next day was packed with programmes and of course, we had chosen everything to do in a leisurely manner, as during my first visit in 1996, we had to visit and see everything hurriedly, due to paucity of time.

The next morning, first we went to the 'Louvre Museum' and our programme's name was 'Walking tour of Louvre'. The private vehicle picked us up from the hotel and dropped us near the Louvre Museum. We were guided to assemble in one particular place and were provided with a pocket-held small ear speaker. We took this tour of more than 2 hours, only because, I had decided to see every aspect of the museum including the world-famous painting of 'Monalisa' in a leisurely manner. To save time, we had preferred to take 'Skip the line tour' with a very small group.

Being one of the largest museums in the world, it had over 35,000 objects on display from prehistory to the 19th century, spread across more than 650,000 square feet of gallery space. Our guide was a lady and she led us through the galleries of extraordinary French institutions and explained the changing face of the Louvre through its architecture and design. The iconic glass pyramid, the art of Jacques-Louis David, Gericault, and Leonardo da Vinci like 'The Venus de Milo', Winged Victory of Samothrace and the most famous 'Mona Lisa' painted by da Vinci, all made the tour of the Louvre very satisfying and educative as well.

After more than 2 hours of walking, we were tired and hungry. We had our lunch and spent some time outside the museum to relax after lunch. We had sufficient time in hand and our next trip was to the Eiffel tower and a cruise ride on the River Seine. First, we went on the cruise ride in River Seine, which was a new experience for Rachita, as I had already gone on the ride in 1996. But then, after 19 years, it was another great experience to have the cruise ride along with wife. We thoroughly enjoyed the ride and then thought of climbing the Eiffel Tower.

The cruise ride point and the Eiffel tower are very close to each other. With our special ticket, it hardly took any time for us to climb the Eiffel tower. We were extremely lucky to climb the Eiffel tower on that day, as just before 2 days only it had opened, after remaining closed for 7 days. There were several pickpocketing incidents and it was shut for seven days, to take precautionary measures. I vividly remember the Eiffel tower was full of 'logos' of the French Open tennis tournament, as French Open was going on in Paris during our visit. The spectacular ascent, a unique panoramic view of Paris, and a glittering beacon in the skies of the Capital were just amazing, and we were enjoying it thoroughly. As we all know, the height of the Eiffel tower is 324mts, the architectural height is 300mts, but the top floor is at a height of 276mts.There, at 276mts, I told the story of my visit to Eiffel tower in 1996 and how Subrat Sen and I had taken beer at that height and enjoyed the evening. At the top floor Rachita and I enjoyed the panoramic view of Paris, thoroughly. We also spent some time on the 2nd and the 1st floor while descending. The breeze that was blowing and the overall experience of climbing the iconic tower was just amazing. By the time we came down, it was around 8 pm and the lighting of the Eiffel tower had not started, as it was supposed to start at around 9 pm after sunset.

Since we had a hectic day, we preferred to go back to the hotel and relax. The next day, our programme was 'Dinner at Eiffel 58' at 7:30 pm, and we were supposed to report to the tourist office by 6 pm.

Hence, for us, the whole day was free and we chose to relax in the hotel. At around one in the afternoon, we simply went for a walk to the 'Champs Elysees' area, as it was walking distance from our hotel. We preferred to have burger and chicken nuggets from McDonald's during lunch. By the time we finished our food and came to the road, there was a huge crowd by the side of the road and the whole length of the road up to 'Arc de Triomphe' was cordoned by police. We asked a policeman, as to why the whole road was cordoned and he replied that The King of Spain would be travelling on that road. Just within a couple of minutes, the King of Spain with full convoy passed through. The fleet of motorcycle guards as well as on horseback were looking magnificent. That was a very rare experience that we could witness. We took several photographs of the elegant sight and after the convoy went forward, we spent some time in the 'Arc de Triomphe' and took a lot of photographs there too.

We then walked for a while and reached our hotel by 3 pm. We took a rest, as the vehicle was supposed to come for a pick up at 5:30 pm for our evening trip to Eiffel tower. We went to the tourist office where we were asked to board a beautiful bus. The bus started at 6:30 pm and we reached the Eiffel tower on time. Again, it was in the skip the line mode and that was always fascinating us, not having to stand in the long queue and wasting time. Our guide was again a smart lady and led us to the restaurant at 58 meters level. When we entered the restaurant, we could not comprehend that it could be so huge and beautiful. The tables were well decorated with a flower vase and 2 wine bottles, one white and the other red wine. We were escorted to our identified table by a smartly dressed and well-mannered waiter. It was a full three-course dinner, with sufficient wine. By the side of our table, a young boy with his father was sitting. We started having a conversation with them and could discover that the old man was a Tennis coach and the young boy was his son. They had come from the USA to enjoy the 'French Open Tennis'. We were the only Indian couple in that group in the restaurant. The food was exotic and better than the food which was served in the 'Lido show'. The best part of the 'Eiffel 58' experience was, that we were having dinner in the world-famous Eiffel Tower and able the see the beautiful view of Paris city through huge glass panes. It was an unforgettable lifetime experience. That dinner of 'Eiffel 58' was worth spending the money.

In the same voucher, we had the ticket for the cruise ride in the River Seine. After dinner, we preferred to go for a cruise ride and not only enjoy the ride again like the previous day but also enjoy the lighting of the Eiffel tower after the sunset. Our guide had informed us that, the bus would go back at 9:30 pm and anyone who wants to continue in the Eiffel tower area, would have to make their own arrangement. We decided to enjoy as much as we could and would go late to the hotel. So, we deliberately moved around and enjoyed the place and sat on the cruise at 9:30 pm. The night ride experience in the cruise was different and we enjoyed the glittering light of the Eiffel tower from our cruise. The lighting that I had seen in 1996 and that I saw in 2015, was a much-improved version. The design of the lighting was changing with each passing minute. Rachita was extremely thrilled to see such a spectacular sight after having dinner at 'Eiffel 58'. By the time, we finished our ride and thoroughly enjoyed the evening, we boarded a cab and went to our hotel. By 11:30 pm, we reached our hotel. That was the last night in Paris and the next day our flight was at 1:30 pm from Chares de Gaulle Airport to New York, USA.

We completed our Europe trip and were discussing our trip to recapitulate the good memories. The overall Europe trip experience, this time was absolutely different, new, and above all very enjoyable, as I wanted to do the unique things, which I was not able to do in my previous visits. First of all, the company of my wife, who is very passionate about Europe, enhanced our enjoyment and we visited every place very leisurely. The unique trips like whisky and waterfall, which was full of tranquillity, in the remote country side of Scotland, the ride in London eye, the Lido show and the dinner at Eiffel -58 in Paris were few exclusive experiences, out of the overall Europe trip. Finally, after having spent so many days in Europe, we were leaving for USA for the second time to visit some new places in a different environment, which was also very exciting for us.

The next day we left the hotel by 9:30 am and as per the programme, the vehicle was available at the hotel on time. By 10:30 am, we were there at the airport and finished our formalities. I bought a Jonny Walker 'Explorer Club' whisky for my co-brother-in-law, Manoj, as we were going to their house in the USA. The flight took off exactly at 1:30 pm for New York and we had a great time on board. Since the flight duration was around 8 hours, we were a bit apprehensive about the aircraft of Air France, through which we flew to New York. To our good luck, it was a Boeing 787 and was extremely comfortable. We were so thrilled and relaxed to sit in the flight that, it cannot be explained. We could see the clouds in the sky and even the runway while landing, on our on-screen display. I was so amazed and asked the air hostess and discovered that the plane had an Enhanced Vision System (EVS). That was absolutely a new experience for us.

Chapter 12:

Leisure and Pleasure in the USA

Finally, we landed at New York JFK airport at around 3 pm (New York time). Since it was the second trip to the same airport, we did not have any problem and came out comfortably after completing the formalities. We hired a cab and went to our hotel, which I had booked earlier and reached at around 5 pm. We were ecstatic to see the room and the location of the hotel, which was just fantastic. In 2007, we had enjoyed New York and had seen all the major places with Nirmal uncle (Mamu). But that was during the daytime and I always desired to see the nightlife and beautiful lighting of New York, for which it is famous. Hence, right from India, while making the planning for the tour, I had booked a decent hotel in New York named 'Belvedere' which was in a central place in 48th street.

Rachita being very social, she keeps in touch with not only family and friends, but also all of our daughters' friends. I knew that 2 of them were married and settled near New York. But it was such a pleasant surprise to me that Rachita had contacted them and within one hour of check in to our hotel, one of them named Monika (I knew her as Duli, as they were our neighbour in Rourkela) with her husband Santosh arrived at our hotel. I met her husband for the first time and was very happy. He was a cool and smart guy. After spending some time in our hotel room and having some coffee, we started our visit to New York City. We boarded a cab and started our journey. Duli and her husband played the role of our guides. We first got down in a marketplace and visited the Manhattan area. Then around 7 pm they suddenly asked us to go to a restaurant. Duli, during her childhood, was our neighbour and a good friend of my elder daughter Anisha. She knew my taste and took us to a beautiful rooftop restaurant. The name of the rooftop restaurant was '230 FIFTH Roof Top' and the restaurant and bar were located on the 20th floor. We had the 360 degrees' view of New York City. Santosh asked about my preference for an alcoholic beverage and we had a couple of beers with several types of food. The best part of the restaurant was that we sat there and saw the skyline of New York City, including the iconic building, 'The Empire State Building'. When we reached the rooftop, it was around 7:15 pm and as dusk approached, the city of New York slowly lit up. The Empire State Building taking the centre stage in its lighting gave a mesmerising sight. The lighting was changing at regular intervals and the sight was all the more spectacular. We spent a wonderful time with Duli and Santosh for more than 3 hours and took several photographs.

We then proceeded to the most happening place 'Times Square'. As such, walking in the streets of New York, the streets full of lights, it was something very unique. But when we reached Times Square, our excitement grew two-folds. With the neon lights and big LED screens and several street shows going on, it was a different atmosphere. The Times Square in the midtown Manhattan section is the most visited tourist attraction in the world. There was a huge LED screen and we stood in front of that, our own image started getting displayed on the screen after just a few seconds. That was an experience that we will never forget.

We were having such a wonderful time that we did not realise that it was already midnight. My sister-in-law had recommended eating street food in that area. We had that food and it was really delicious. Though we were enjoying every moment, we were tired, because of the time zone change from Paris to New York. We then decided to disperse and Duli & Santosh boarded a metro and went to Jersey City which was 45 minutes away from New York. We then boarded a cab and went back to our hotel. By the time we reached our hotel, it was around 1:30 am. The next morning, we boarded a bus from New York and travelled to Washington DC, as recommended by my sister-in-law Ishita. The 4 hours journey by bus was very nice. It was a nonstop bus, provided with a beautiful washroom facility. After we reached Washington DC, we boarded a metro and went to Gaithersburg. Manoj and Ishita welcomed us very warmly and we reached their house within 15 minutes. It was such a warm and nostalgic feeling to see them again in USA, when we finally reached their house. It was a different house from the one we had visited in 2007. Location-wise, the new house was just great. We were so tired of travelling in Europe and New York, that we wanted to chill for 2 to 3 days and not move long distances. During that period, both the children of Ishita & Manoj were at home. The elder one, the son Sidhant, who was perusing engineering at Cornell University of Engineering and the younger one, the daughter, who was studying in tenth grade. We were enjoying with the children at home and I was playing video game with Sidhant, which was very thrilling.

On the third day, we visited 'The Great falls of the Potomac'. It was at the border of Maryland and Virginia. The series of waterfalls were so beautifully falling into the river Potomac. The scenic view of the falls was just amazing during dusk. We sat on a rock and enjoyed some snacks and then came back home. The other place that we visited after three days of our arrival, was Rio, which we had visited last time in 2007. The other day Manoj took me to a huge liquor shop. We bought a crate of 'Corona Extra' and 'Stella Artois' beer each and came home. The next morning, being a Sunday, we went to the Farmer's market. It was one of its kind and I could not visualize that such markets could also exist in the USA. We brought several vegetables including a typical lemon and some garlic. We came home and Manoj gave me a small surprise. Before lunch, he opened the Corona Extra beer bottle and squeezed a small piece of lemon that we bought from Farmer's market, and offered me the bottle. It was very soothing and tasty. Though I had tried several types of beer including 'Corona Extra' earlier, drinking Corona Extra beer with a typical smelling lemon was a first-time experience.

The next week on Tuesday we went to Washington DC with Ishita, as Manoj went to his office. At that time the Smithsonian area was under renovation and as such, we had visited all museums, and Imax, etc., during the 2007 visit. So, we preferred to visit the World War II Memorial, Lincoln Memorial, and Washington Memorial. All these places are of historical importance and the whole area is well-maintained with fountains, a lake, and an all-over beautiful grass lawn with landscaping. That fascinated us a lot. We bought several souvenirs from a beautiful shop which also had a restaurant. After a 3-hour walk, we were tired and had our food there. Ishita, gifted me a beautiful cap with a Logo of Washington DC. That is still my most favourite cap even after six years. We came back home after a beautiful qualitatively spent day. By the time we reached home, Manoj had already come back from his office. He was busy preparing food. He was preparing Biriyani and I asked him if he was tired. He replied with a smile, "Boss Ye to mera Stress Buster Hai", it meant that cooking was his stress buster. That statement fascinated me. We had some pegs of Scotch Whisky and enjoyed the food.

During our dinner, we planned for our trip to Miami on that Saturday. The planning part was very interesting and great. Even in the 2007 visit, we had visited Canada with Manoj's SUV and we made a similar planning to hop to different places and reach the destination. Our planning was almost over and we also finished our dinner. The next day we did not go anywhere and simply chilled at home. The other day, which was a Thursday, we went to Hagerstown for shopping and it was a nice day spent with several shopping. On Friday, Ishita and Manoj had invited their close friends' group for dinner, in our honour. Right from the morning, multiple food preparations had started, both for the evening dinner and for our next day's trip to Miami.

By 7:30 pm all their friends started coming with different varieties of Indian food and dessert. In the evening, it was worth seeing the spread of different kinds of food. Manoj had brought a 'Glenfiddich' whisky bottle and the one that I had taken, which was a Jonny Walker 'Explorer Series', everything was opened. We had a great time and I could meet many of Manoj's friends. Among all those, I developed a friendship with one gentleman named Dr. Rao. He worked as a genetic scientist. There were two reasons for my friendship with him. First of all, he hailed from a nearby place of Rourkela called Purnapani, as his father was working in those mines. He spent his childhood in that place and could relate to Rourkela and could speak in Odia. Secondly, he was a frequent traveller and had travelled all over the globe, which is my passion too. I am still in touch with him and he has visited my house at Rourkela, too, after that visit to USA. That evening was wonderful. It was at around 11:30 pm that the party started dispersing and we all slept at around 1 am on that day.

Manoj was on leave for the next whole week and we were not in a hurry to start early the next day, that being a Saturday and a holiday. We got up late and leisurely started around noon on Saturday, for our long journey to Miami, Florida. Our nephew, Sidhant, stayed back at home, as he was supposed to go back to his hostel, the next day and join his classes from Monday. Hence, except Sidhant, the five of us moved on Saturday. Since it was the month of June, the climate was awesome. Our SUV was full of food and drinks with an icebox. We had our lunch in a Mexican restaurant around 4 pm. After that, we went to the high way rest room and took a rest for some time. We also moved about the inside of the whole area. It was very astonishing to see dispenser-based unmanned counters for food and beverages. The most unique one was the Ice cream counter. With the advent of technology, the machine was operating through "Robot". We simply inserted money and the arm of the Robot opened the lid of the ice cream box and picked the one that we had chosen and dispensed it to us. It was a unique experience for me and I was more fascinated to see how from 2007 to 2015 the technology had become so advanced.

Again, leisurely, we started our long journey. Manoj had booked the hotel in a resort called St. Augustine. The distance from Manoj's place at Gaithersburg to St. Augustine was around 760 miles and we had estimated to reach there by midnight. We travelled quite leisurely through Virginia, South Carolina, and Georgia. It was an amazing experience to travel on that road. We were so hungry that around 10 pm we stopped our car in a remote place and had food that Ishita had packed at home. We had a lot of cooked, semi-cooked, and ready-to-eat food in our car.

We relaxed for 30 minutes and again proceeded. We reached St. Augustine at around 1 am in the night and straight went to the hotel. We checked in and again had some refreshments and slept. The next morning, we went to the places of visit nearby. We found that, historically the place had a lot of importance, which of course Manoj knew earlier and had chosen that place for a halt. The place was originally a Spanish colony, on the northeast coast of Florida. This small city is USA's oldest city which offers more than just the charming cobblestone streets, historical landmarks, and pristine beaches. We saw the whole place and found that the city is a well-preserved example of Spanish-style buildings and 18th and 19th-century architecture. Since it was a walkable city with oceanfront parks, we thoroughly enjoyed the place.

We had our booking in Hotel Hilton in Miami and proceeded towards Miami after seeing St. Augustine. The distance from St. Augustine to Miami is around 330 miles and that would take around 4 and ½ hours to reach. We started around 12:30 pm. It was around that time that Rachita, got a message on her mobile. It was surprising to get a message from one of our neighbour's sons. Rachita, always keeps in touch with old friends and their families. She had simply posted photographs of St. Augustine on Facebook and that was seen by a friend's son Srivasth and he immediately contacted us. We knew that he lived in the USA but had no idea, which part of USA. It was so nice and thrilling to know that he lived in West Palm Beach which fell on the way of our journey. He invited us for lunch at an Indian restaurant and we accepted his invitation, knowing fully well, that we would be having late lunch. We were also very excited to meet him and his family in the USA. He was also very thrilled to know that we are joining them for lunch. The only issue was that, we had left St. Augustine around 12:30 pm and we planned to reach Miami as early as possible in the evening. But we could not resist the excitement of meeting Srivatsh after more than a decade. The distance to West Palm Beach was around 250 miles and we reached at around 4 pm at the restaurant that had been decided upon. The name of the restaurant was 'Indus Indian & Herbal Cuisine'. It was a beautiful restaurant with a beautiful garden and a lot of creepers. After having varieties of draught and bottled beers, we found our Indian 'Kingfisher' lager beer there in that restaurant. It was so fascinating to drink Kingfisher beer after more than a month. We had a great time there and spent more than an hour in that place.

We again proceeded towards Miami and covered a distance of around 80 miles and reached our hotel 'Hilton' with n one and half hours. It was at 7 pm that we reached our hotel. It was a fantastic hotel with all facilities and the best part was that the sea beach was only at a 10 minutes' walking distance. Immediately after checking in, we decided to walk to the sea beach. By 7:30 pm, we were on the sea beach and enjoyed thoroughly. We did not take bath in the sea, keeping it for the next day, as we had a 3-day programme in Miami. The sunset started around 8:15 pm and it was a beautiful scene that we saw and after it was dark, we walked on the street near the beach. It was truly a happening place with several restaurants and full of light. Different coloured and typically dressed girls were walking as well as on open cars with full blast music. It was a unique experience to move in the streets. We did not keep a long programme in the evening on that day and came back to our hotel on the first day at around 10 pm.

The next morning, we enquired in the travel desk of our hotel in Hilton about the local tour. The person gave several brochures and we selected the 'Everglades Mangrove Airboat Tour'. We had an awesome breakfast with a fantastic spread and then got ready for our tour. We waited in the lobby and the bus picked us up at 10 am and we proceeded to the spot. We boarded the boat with the guide and the guide was narrating the whole journey. The boat was zipping through twisting mangrove tunnels. The unique evergreen plants and animals that we could see with the wind on the face were very exciting. After enjoying the tour seeing alligators and birds, we were taken to a reptile zoo. We saw many baby alligators and snakes with a big Python snake show.

We came back after a good day and had our lunch on the way. Finally, we reached our hotel at around 3 pm. We took a rest and were ready for our visit to Miami beach in the evening. Around 5 pm, we were fully prepared to have fun in the world-famous Miami beach. The beach was a bit crowded, but gradually people who had spent the whole day started leaving and we enjoyed ourselves more on the beach with less crowd. There were lifeguards available up to 8 pm and we merrily bathed in the sea up to that time. It was such a unique experience with the white sand and shallow water beach.

After enjoying in the seawater, we had a plain water bath in the beautiful wash rooms made for the visitors, just by the side of the beach. After that, we wanted to enjoy some beverages and food in the nearby open-garden restaurants. The place was full of life and the restaurants were full of creepers and flowers. We sat outside of the restaurant and ordered 'Calamari' and 'Mojito'. We were served with 1 litre of Mojito in a big bowl with several straws. It was very interesting to see the bowl served to us. The drink was very tasty and thereafter, we ordered the crab and other seafood, which was very famous there. In fact, after dinner, we again moved around the streets. It was full of sparkling lights and by then the area became very crowded. It was altogether a different experience, to see the activities in that area with young people dancing in front of the restaurants. We then went to another lively joint and had a beer and the ladies wanted to have some ice cream. After having spent some time there, it was already 11 pm and we decided to go back to the hotel.

The next morning, we first went to a place called 'Little Havana'. It was a replica of Cuba and the Latin rhythm could be felt in that place. The place was full of lively markets and the unmistakable smell of cigars. It was quite easy to navigate our way in Little Havana. We could enjoy the area's street life, booming Cuban music, and the lively coffee shops were open round the clock. The music from the bars and restaurant was just great and we felt like dancing. Finally, we went to a big store having several types of souvenirs and the best part of that store was that several varieties of cigars were made and sold there. Though I am not a smoker, I bought a pack of cigars and Rachita bought some souvenirs for our family. It was a unique experience to visit and spend time at Little Havana.

After the visit to Little Havana, we went to the Miami Harbour and enjoyed the cruise ride in the sea. The name of the tour was 'Island Queen Cruise & Tour'. It was about an hour's tour and there was a beautiful bar inside the cruise. I had a beer and developed a friendship with many of our co-passengers. It was an amazing experience on the cruise to see all the beautiful big houses of celebrities like singer Gloria Estefan, actor Sylvester Stallone, and all the other rich people's houses. The narration in the cruise by the guide was just great. After spending a beautiful time, we came back to the hotel and after taking a rest, we again got prepared for bathing in the Miami beach. We enjoyed ourselves the same way and we spent more time in the sea, that day. I remember it was the 14th of June 2015 and, on that day, we went to the hotel at 1 am after thoroughly enjoying the beach area of Miami.

Though the distance to our hotel was only a 10 minutes' walk, we still preferred to go by cab, as it was a bit late. We boarded 2 cabs and reached our Hilton hotel. The next day, we had the programme to go to Key West in the same state of Florida. We started very leisurely the next day and wanted to enjoy the drive from Miami to Key West. The distance was around 170 miles and we should have reached within 3 to 3 ½ hours. But we knew that the drive itself would be nice and enjoyable. We started around 11.30am and drove very slowly and hopped in several places on the way. First, we stopped at Islamorada Beer Company, which was a yellow building. There was a distillery adjoining the beer company. It was fun to try some of the beers that included regional ingredients and a local flare. Then we had a late lunch in the Atlantic Edge restaurant, which was a beautiful property with great views of the sea. We were continuously on the GPS, trying to find out what would be the next worth visiting place before we reach Key West.

We then came across one of the most impressive bridges named 'Seven-mile bridge'. It was a lifetime experience to drive across the 7 miles long bridge across the sea. The uniqueness of the bridge was that it is so long and straight that we could not even see the end of the bridge. It was a beautiful sight to see that the sea touches the bridge and also the mirage feeling was just awesome. We finally reached Key West and checked in to a hotel named 'Parrot Key Hotel & Villas'. The time that we arrived was around 8:30 pm and it was already dark. We were extremely tired and after checking into the hotel, I and Manoj went around the hotel and saw the beautiful swimming pool and the poolside bar. We both were extremely tired and jumped into the swimming pool and had some round of Cuban rum. The ambience of the swimming pool area with a beautiful garden, with palm and coconut trees, was just great. We had our final round of rum after swimming in the pool and then had our dinner.

The next day, we proceeded to the southernmost point of the USA, which is a very popular place to visit. There is a big landmark by the side of the sea, which writes '90 Miles to Cuba, Southernmost Point, Continental USA'. It was a great place to spend some time by the side of the sea and get some breeze. We were very thirsty and had green coconut water. The hawker was having a portable drilling machine and unlike cutting the outer shell, a hole was made with the drilling machine and we drank the coconut water with a straw. It was something very new and innovative that I saw for the first time in my life. After spending some time, we had a beer with snacks at a beautiful street famous for pubs. It was Duval Street where we enjoyed our beer and food and then came back to our hotel. We took a rest to prepare ourselves to enjoy again in the evening.

Our evening destination was the famous Mallory Square. Around 6 pm we started for the place. The uniqueness of that place was view of the sunset. It was a happening place and we enjoyed the sunset at around 7:30 pm and thereafter I and Manoj went to the adjacent bars. Live music was making that place very vibrant. We had Cuban rum and danced to glory with the local music. Another typical fresh pineapple drink was available, which was very famous. The ladies wanted to have that pineapple drink. The outer shell of the pineapple would remain intact and they would scoop out and remove the inside pulpy portion, out of which, they made juice and again put it inside the outer shell and serve for drinking. It was such an awesome drink, both look and taste wise, that the ladies enjoyed it to the brim. Gradually the place became very crowded and more enjoyable. Sitting in a restaurant eating with the whole family, became difficult. But since right from 6 pm we were enjoying ourselves there, it was not very difficult to get a space.

We enjoyed ourselves up to 10:30 pm there and came back to the hotel. It was indeed a well-spent day and finally, our preparation for the return journey to Gaithersburg started. As we were having our own vehicle, there was no hurry, and the next morning, we got ready very leisurely. In the process of travelling to different places in Key West, we had not gone to the beautiful beach, right in front of our hotel. So, after getting ready, we went to the sea beach and enjoyed there for more than an hour. We finally started around noon from Key West, for our return journey.

The total distance from Key West to Gaithersburg, Maryland was around 1250 miles and the time it would have taken was around 19 to 20 hours. It was virtually impossible and very difficult to drive at a stretch that too such a long distance. We decided to stay back for a night on the way. We checked in to a hotel at around 9 pm and spent the night there. The next morning, after breakfast we proceeded for Gaithersburg, Maryland. The journey was again great, passing through the countryside, as Manoj decided to go on a different route to have a different experience. We reached home around 10 pm and were extremely tired. We took rest that night and the next day also we did not go anywhere and simply chilled at home.

Our return journey was scheduled on on 22nd June and we had only 3 to 4 days to spend in the USA. The next day again we went to the Rio area and the best place to spend quality time with all facilities in place. We did our last-minute shopping and were thinking of the long duration of the return journey. The next day, we were invited by one of Manoj's friends named Shrikanth. We all went for lunch and met his wife and parents also. As a music lover, he had a fantastic surround sound system with an antique gramophone. He started playing some

Hindi songs with an old LP record. I was a bit surprised to see and listen to music in such a system. The actual surprise came when he showed his all-old record collection. In some record covers, I found my and my wife's signature. My sister-in-law Ishita then revealed that she had taken those records from us from India and had gifted it to Srikanth. The more surprising part was that the normal CDs were costing only $6 to $10, whereas, the old LP records were costing $40 to $60 in the USA at that time. We had a great time on that day at Srikanth's place and came home after the evening coffee.

The next day we did all our packing and our face became gloomy to think that on 22nd June our return flight was there from Dulles airport. It was again British Airways and Ishita dropped us at the airport. We were lucky to have no overweight charge for our luggage which was within the limit, as per the norm of British Airways. Our flight was scheduled from Dulles to Heathrow, London. It was a double-decker aircraft, which was an Airbus 380. Our seat was allotted on the upper deck and it was a new experience for us to sit on the upper deck. More than 500 passengers were there in the aircraft. Our flight was scheduled at 5 pm and after boarding and settling down in the aircraft, again we started thinking about our home in India and it was a mixed feeling of leaving the USA and the enjoyment for last more than one month. At the same time, we wanted to reach home, as early as possible. We reached Heathrow at around 5 am (London time). The layover at Heathrow was for about 4 hours. We freshened up and the British Airlines gave us a breakfast coupon as we were coming to Delhi again by British airways. We again boarded the flight at 9 am and reached New Delhi at around 10:30 pm.

We completed our formalities and came to the duty-free shop. In fact, during our onward journey, I had booked some alcohol including a 'Johnny Walker Blue Label', as there were good schemes and if someone pre-books it, it is much cheaper, if you buy it on arrival. I collected those articles and came out of the airport. My daughter Anooja and nephew Saurav were waiting for us outside the airport. It was very nostalgic to land in the homeland and meet Saurav and Anooja after a month. We went to Saurav's house at Gurugram. We took out all the gifts, etc., and by the time we slept, it was 3 am. Somehow, to my bad luck, my jet lag started and I did not get any sleep. After 2 days we came to Rourkela via Ranchi and reached home after 40 days. That was the longest trip that we ever had on our foreign tour. Rachita joined her school and I joined my plant duty. It was extremely difficult to adjust for few days in the plant environment and that too with the severe jet lag, which continued for almost a week. Thereafter, life became normal.

Chapter 13:

Superannuation, Portugal, and A Spanish Delight

It was the end of June 2015; I became the acting Head of Department once again for more than six months. That was another unique opportunity and experience to take up more challenges and responsibility. However, I started learning further about steel making and also delivered talks at NIT, Rourkela, several times in different events including National seminars. Such talks were possible at NIT, Rourkela because of Academia & Industry relationship under "Technology Innovation and Industrial Relations" scheme. Having delivered, several talks at NIT, Rourkela, it boosted my confidence and subsequently, one of the professors approached me for writing a book along with him about the practical aspect, challenges and its solution through modelling, of steelmaking. It was something that fascinated me, but I could not decide immediately and asked for some time to think over the offer, as it was a very difficult and challenging job.

As my superannuation was in May'2018, for me one of the most important activities was to get my younger daughter Anooja married. We coaxed her to marry a bit early, so that, much before my superannuation, we will be relieved of our primary responsibilities. She was doing a very decent job as a lawyer at Gurugram and we also got the news about her boyfriend, who was also a lawyer. She finally agreed to marry but only in December 2016. We agreed to her proposal and began a dialogue with the groom's side, who belonged to Kolkata. They also accepted the proposal.

Then we decided the ring ceremony to be held at Kolkata in April 2016. We made all the preparations and along with my close family members and friends, about 20 people, went to Kolkata for the ring ceremony. Very nice arrangements were made by them and we performed all the rituals and puja needed for the ring ceremony and they hosted a beautiful lunch. The same evening, we had a party again with our friends and family. We then planned a trip in May 2016 to Bangalore to visit Anisha & Anil's place for planning and shopping, including the making of the invitation card. Anil being in the creative field, designed the invitation card. Anooja came from Gurugram and we spent more than 1 week in Bangalore together.

The marriage was scheduled for the 13th of December. We had a cocktail party at Hotel Radhika and Sangeet at our house. The marriage was held on the 13th morning and the reception party in the evening at Indo German club. Our family and friends came from all parts of India and had a great time. It was a memorable event for all of us. We were then invited to Kolkata for our groom Barganil side's reception on 16th December. That was held in a resort by the side of the Ganga River and was very well organised. We reached Rourkela on the 18th morning and felt very lonely, after such a grand function.

After a couple of days, the winter festival started at Indo German club and we enjoyed those few days up to the new year. However, just after that, once I started attending my office, the promotion aspect started sinking in, which was due from the 30th of June 2016. But then, I had forgotten about it, as I was extremely busy with my daughter's wedding. In February 2017, the promotion order came out and to my surprise, I was promoted to the post of General Manager. I was in seventh heaven and felt that at least before my superannuation in May 2018, I became the General Manager. I was thankful to God, my parent, and my organisation, for having been promoted to that post.

Since it was a new area for me after promotion, I had to slog a lot to learn and adjust to the new environment in the Refractory department. Within two months I could adjust and started enjoying the new challenges. In the meantime, I decided and had started writing the book with Professor Snehanshu of NIT Rourkela, who had requested me earlier to become the co-author of a book. In addition to my normal assignment, it was extremely difficult to write about steelmaking, and I had also started writing an article on Secondary Metallurgy simultaneously. I would go to NIT Rourkela, after my plant working hours, around 7-8 pm. I would sit in the laboratory, sometimes up to 10-11 pm to write, for more than six months. I never expected that I could write an article for an international journal and the book simultaneously. However, with a lot of effort, it got completed in November'2017. My target was to get the book and the article published, before my superannuation on 31st May 2018. I felt extremely accomplished to have both published in May 2018. This was possible only because of the constant support and encouragement from Professor Snehanshu and NIT, Rourkela authorities. Even during my farewell, all those achievements were cited and I truly felt accomplished. By then, I had decided to pursue further writing technical articles and also take classes in different institutes and organisations. Right from the beginning, I had decided not to join any Steel Industry, though I had good offers in hand, but preferred to become a free-lance consultant and a writer. I still feel that writing a technical book titled "Process modelling for steel industry" is one of the greatest achievements in my life.

As, I was going to superannuate in May'2018, another great passion, which is travelling, triggered in my mind and I discussed with Rachita about visiting some place abroad within Asia, just after my superannuation. In fact, our last visit was before 3 years and we had not travelled abroad after June '2015. She was always interested to go different parts of Europe, but not Asia. One fine morning, she suddenly mentioned for a tour to Spain in Europe, which of course I had not travelled to and it appealed me. I agreed and wanted to discuss with other friends, who could join us in June 2018. In the same month, at a certain marriage reception party, I raised this travel plan in the presence of my friends and their spouses. My childhood friends Subrat and Deepak showed interest, who were also working as engineers in Rourkela Steel Plant, like me. Deepak's wife Tanusri, who is a professor in English, was very happy about the proposal and wanted to add Portugal along with Spain to our itinerary. Subrat's wife Sumitra, who is a Doctor was also extremely happy about our Spain and Portugal combination tour. We all were very happy and the proposal was accepted by all of us. It was the 3rd week of January and the very next day I called up Mr. Nayak, the franchise owner of M/s Cox and Kings, and went to his office for the preliminary discussion. Like other times, I had done a lot of research about Portugal and Spain. As such, I keep on watching the channel 'Travel XP' on the TV, which is one of my favourite channels, that helps in getting a real feel of different tourist places. I also tried to find out from other sources about the places of our interest in Spain and Portugal. Hence, I gave a tentative plan to Mr. Nayak for a more than 2 weeks programme on the scheme 'Flexi Holidays'. It was not a normally conducted package tour, as I wanted the tour to be exclusive for the six of us. There were several rounds of discussions, when Subrat and Deepak also participated and our itinerary was finalised. We made necessary advance payments for the air tickets and the booking of hotels, etc.

As, I was going to superannuate on the 31st of May, 2018, I wanted to leave Rourkela, the very next day i.e., on the 1st of June. Subrat and Deepak agreed and we made our itinerary accordingly to fly from Mumbai to Lisbon, Portugal. I attended my farewell function on 31st May and on the 1st June, we first went to Bhubaneswar in the evening by Rajya Rani Express. The same evening, we flew to Mumbai. My nephew, Anshu, who is a bank manager came to the airport along with his wife Saswati and we went to his house. The next day our flight to Lisbon was scheduled at 1 am. We had a good time at our Anshu's house. Deepak and Subrat also stayed with their relatives. The next morning, we discussed the meeting point and time at the Mumbai International Airport. We all were very excited about our trip as all of us were friends right from childhood.

Rachita and I went to the market along with my nephew Anshuman and Saswati for some last-minute purchases for our two weeks' tour. After that, we went to a nice restaurant nearby and had good Mughlai food. We came home and started our final packing. I talked to Subrat and Deepak to meet at 10 pm at the airport in Mumbai, right in front of the entrance gate, as our flight was scheduled at 1 am by Air France. All of us met at the designated place on time and there was a smile on everybody's face. We finished our formalities and we had sufficient time in hand to go round the duty-free shops. We bought some chocolates and liquor bottles for our consumption during the tour. We boarded the flight and were very excited about our tour. We, three friends, sat in one place and row and our spouses sat together in a different row. We had some snacks and a couple of drinks on the flight and preferred to sleep early. Our flight duration was of around 9 hours and at around 7 am we reached Charles de Gaulle Airport, Paris. We all were very excited to land in Paris and for me and Rachita, it was 3rd and 2nd time respectively to see the airport. It's a huge airport and our next flight was scheduled at 1 pm Paris time from terminal 2. Hence, we preferred to go directly to Terminal 2 from Terminal 1. We all had a priority pass of our credit cards and went straight to the lounge to get freshened up and take a rest for the next flight.

We got ready by 9:30 am and had some food in the lounge itself. We also got some food of our choice from other kiosks and relaxed in the lounge. Our friend Deepak went outside the lounge and preferred to sleep in a leaning chair. Around 11 am Subrat and I had some beer available in the lounge. At 11:30 am there was an announcement for us to go to the security check for boarding. We thought Deepak would be sleeping somewhere nearby, but could not locate him. All five of us were a bit worried and started searching for him. Finally, Subrat located him sleeping in an open area at a little distance. However, we immediately rushed to the security check and except for Deepak and Tanu, all four of us went to the other side waiting for Deepak and Tanusri to come. To our surprise, Tanusri had kept the passports and did not get them for a moment in her bag. At one point of time, we even thought of postponing the programme. Then Rachita came near Tanusri with permission of the security, though she had crossed the security gate. She asked Tanusri to take out everything from her bag and finally, both the passports could be traced, which were there in her handbag. After having so much anxiety and stress, it was a big relief for all of us. We all virtually ran to the aircraft for boarding, due to the paucity of time. We felt relaxed after such an episode. We were exhausted by then and asked for water in the aircraft, immediately after boarding.

The flight duration was around 2hrs 30 minutes and we reached Lisbon at around 2:30 pm (Lisbon time). The airport was very clean but quite small as compared to Paris. We came out from the airport and saw our driver with the placard. He was wearing a black suit and was very courteous. He led us to a big black Mercedes SUV. Since I had that experience earlier, I had talked about the vehicle to Subrat and Deepak. Both of them were extremely happy to sit in the vehicle which took us to the hotel. We checked in to our pre-booked 4-star hotel, which was centrally located. After settling down and taking a rest, around 5 pm we came for an outing in the nearby places to have a feel of the place. The climate was just great and we walked through the streets and enjoyed it thoroughly. Around 7 pm we felt hungry and went to a beautiful restaurant near our hotel. We had varieties of food including grilled chicken, fish and chips etc. accompanied by red wine.

We took several photographs and at around 9:30 pm came to the hotel and slept.

The next day after having a nice breakfast with varieties of spread, we got ready for our day tour of Lisbon. Again, the black Mercedes SUV came to drop us near the main bus stand. We had our 24-hour pre-booked ticket of the 'hop on hop off' bus for the tour. We all were in a fantastic state of mind as that was the first day of the Lisbon tour. On the very first morning, while travelling in the hop on hop off bus, we found that Lisbon is a vibrant and charismatic city, and one of the finest capital cities in Europe. The city boasts a glorious climate, historic monuments, and a range of activities that fascinated us.

First, we went to the Castelo de Sao Jorge castle, which stands majestically above central Lisbon and is entwined in the early history of Portugal. It was in Lisbon that the Christian crusaders defeated the Moors in 1147. The Portuguese survived a siege by Castile around 1373, and was in the seat of power for Portugal for over 400 years. It was beautiful spot to visit. Then we went to 'Torre de Belem' which is the tourist icon of Lisbon and a beautiful example of the Manueline style of architecture. It is situated on the bank of the Tagus River. It was at around noon and we enjoyed walking through the site with the cold breeze blowing from the river. The Belem Tower is also an UNESCO World Heritage site. There are Arabic-inspired watchtowers, and even the earliest stone statue of a Rhino, in that area. After thoroughly enjoying that place, we decided to go to the Royal Palace. We could not go to the 'Cristo Rei statue' towers above the southern banks of the Tejo Estuary due to paucity of time.

But from the Belem Tower, the 'Cristo Rei statue' was visible on the other side of the Tagus River, above the hills. The Cristo Rei Statue is one of the most prominent monuments in Lisbon. This statue has many similarities to the Christ the Redeemer statue in Rio de Janeiro, in South America, and this is true as the Brazilian monument inspired the Portuguese statue. Apart from being a distinctive landmark, the Cristo Rei statue provides one of the best viewpoints of Lisbon, with unrivalled views of the suspension bridge and city. It was a beautiful sight which we enjoyed from a distance. We did not go near it as we preferred to go to the Lisbon harbour side to have seafood, which is famous for. However, we could capture many photographs of the statue through my camera.

We went to the harbour side by bus, since we had the 24 hours' open bus ticket, and reached there around 3 pm. The Doca do Alcantara harbour was very beautiful with fishing boats and the green water of the sea. The walking pavement was very clean and there were very nice restaurants nearby. We were very thirsty and hungry, as we had travelled for the whole day. We immediately ordered water and beer, followed by seafood, which we had decided to eat right from the morning. Fresh and live seafood were on display and we immediately ordered those, the speciality being lobster. We had a fantastic time having nice seafood. The best part was the ambience and the climate. We could see the beauty of the harbour and simultaneously had our sumptuous lunch. By the time we finished our lunch, it was around 5 pm, and we preferred to go back to our hotel. We took a rest up to 8 pm and again, went for a light dinner at the nearby restaurant. It was a lovely day spent in Lisbon and the next day we had the plan to go to Porto by Train "Alfa Pendular".

There were two different train services between Porto to Lisbon, which are the Intercedes (intercity) and the Alfa Pendular. The Alfa Pendular service is faster and offers a high standard of comfort and facilities like Free WIFI and more legroom etc., but is more expensive than the older intercedes trains. We had our pre-booked tickets in first class, which we had booked earlier in the 'Alfa Pendular' train. It took around 3 hours to cover the 320 km route north from the capital Lisbon to Porto Campanha Station. The train was a super-fast train and the sight during our journey was just great, having mountains and a beautiful landscape. I explored whether the pantry car had the provision of alcoholic beverages or not I had the experience of having beer in the train from Dusseldorf to Berlin in Germany and in London while travelling to Edinburg in the UK. When I found that it was available, I immediately called my friends Deepak and Subrat and had beer and some snacks in the pantry. That overall journey experience from Lisbon to Porto was just amazing.

We reached Porto at around 11:30 am and when came out of the station, we found our driver who was also our guide. He was a very talkative and interesting person. By the time we boarded the vehicle for the sightseeing, it was around noon and we were feeling hungry. The guide took us to a beautiful restaurant and we had lunch, outside the restaurant under the big umbrellas, which is something very common in any part of Europe. After having a great traditional lunch, we started our day visit.

Of all the cities in Portugal, the capital Lisbon is often the favourite, but Porto is the destination of choice and before leaving India we had done some research about the place. Though Porto is smaller in size, but had several attractions with some historical importance. First of all, it's the home of port and the wine cellars in Vila Nova de Gaia which are a must-visit and must-taste joint. Secondly, its Ribeira district is one of the most beautiful historic quarters in the Porto area. Also, like Lisbon, this northern city is hilly, but there are heaps of heavenly parks where we could take a breather. In Porto, we got an extraordinary view of the Douro River, which could be crossed by the iconic Dom Luis iron bridge which connected Porto to Gaia. We visited 'Clerigos Tower' of the city of Porto, which is the city's most iconic silhouette. It was opened in 1763 and is blessed with a beautiful barrage of Baroque motifs. This was designed by an Italian designer Nicolau Nasoni. Given its prominent position, from there, we could see some amazing 360° views of the city from the top.

Next, we went to 'Riberra', which was a Unesco World Heritage Site. After this visit, we went to Foz, which is almost a mini-city within Porto. In the nineteenth century, it was a seaside resort and nowadays also, it is a beach resort for tourists. We then went to the 'Serra do Pilar' before the visit to the wine cellar. The Serra do Pilar is a jagged hill above the Douro River on the Gaia side. Needless to say, that the view of the river was spectacular, especially at sunset. Our next visit was to a wine cellar, which we knew, would be very enjoyable. We knew a bit of the history, but our motive was to have a real feel. Port Wine is born in the Douro Valley, but it is the city of Porto that gives the name to the wine. Because that's where the wine ages and is shipped from here to all over the world. We had read that a visit to the Port wine cellars is a mandatory activity during any trip to Porto.

These Port wine cellars were all located across the river from the old city centre of Porto and to get there, we crossed the emblematic Dom Luis bridge. It took us about 10 minutes and we easily walked from one side to the other. Nearly all Port wine cellars provide guided tours and tastings. There were dozens of Port wine cellars and we selected the one which was suggested by our guide. We went to the cellar 'Caves Ferreira' which was the only big house of Port Wine that has remained in Portuguese hands since its foundation. Founded in 1751, the brand's history is intertwined with the history of the evolution of the Douro Region. By visiting Caves Ferreira, we discovered a brand that is over 250 years old, the history of Port wine and the Douro region. We found huge wooden casks, almost of room size. We tasted several types of Port wine and also bought a bottle of wine each, with a different flavour. The wine cellar visit, which we deliberately kept at the last, was worth it. It was an amazing experience in the city of Porto and by the time we finished our wine tour, it was almost 6 pm. We then went straight to the railway station to board our train for the return journey at 7 pm. We reached Lisbon around 10 pm and were extremely tired. We simply slept that night, as our next day's journey was scheduled at 2 pm to Madrid, Spain by flight.

The next morning, we got up leisurely and had our sumptuous breakfast with pleasure, as we were supposed to go to the airport around 11:30 am from our hotel. We reached the airport around 11:45 am and after finishing the formalities, we were waiting to board the flight at 1:30 pm. The best surprise was that we were going to meet our elder daughter, Anisha, and son-in-law, Anil, in Madrid. Anisha had gone to London on her office work for a month and she went to Spain on holiday directly from London. Anil had joined her in Spain, after flying from India. We had this information only before our travel, as they intended to surprise us. It was a pleasant coincidence that they had extensively travelled through Spain, starting from Seville in down south, Barcelona, and several other places. They had travelled by a self-driven car. Their final destination was Madrid, where they were there for the last three days and knew all the happening and good things about Madrid. They were simply waiting to meet us in Madrid.

We reached Madrid by flight at around 4 pm and immediately rushed to our hotel. Anisha and Anil's hotel was very near to ours and they simply walked to our hotel within 15 minutes of our arrival. We were extremely happy to meet them in a foreign land and it was our good luck that we could spend a couple of hours in Madrid with them. It was such a joyful moment for us and they first took us to a happening place full of food and fun. The place was nothing but a fantastic traditional Spanish eating joint. The name of the place was 'Mercado de San Miguel'. It was the most popular market in Madrid among tourists, since it is located in the centre of Madrid. It was around 20 minutes' walk from our hotel. We were very lucky that Anisha and Anil took us there as they had already had a great experience of that place. Several varieties of traditional tapas with olive were available with many types of seafood, beer, and wine. We thoroughly enjoyed that place and ate different varieties of tapas and other foods. We took several photographs and finally Anisha had to leave for her return journey to New Delhi, India from Madrid airport. Her flight was scheduled at 11 pm and she enjoyed with us up to 7:30 pm. Anil went to see her off at the airport and again came back to the same place. We had some draught beers and had food, up to 9:30 pm. It was a very enjoyable evening.

However, our enjoyment did not stop there. Anil took us to a typical place to have Chocolate and Churro, which is a famous sweet dish of Spain. The place was in so much demand that we had to stand in the queue to get a table. Finally, Anil managed to get a table and we had the Churro and the Hot chocolate, which was the combination meant for eating. It was just an awesome experience to have that sweet dish at Madrid. Finally, around 10:30 pm we were returning to the hotel and found a lively place where a lot of live music, dance, acrobatics, and fire juggling was going on. We spent some time there and then proceeded to our hotel. By the time we reached our hotel, it was around midnight. The next day Anil had his flight at 7 am from Madrid airport to Bangalore. We had the programme of sightseeing of Madrid by hop on and hop off bus the next day.

After our breakfast, we started our sightseeing tour of Madrid. We knew Madrid is a city so full of life and culture that it's hard to do justice to it in a few paragraphs. Artistically, the city has a different significance against any city in Europe, with the best art museums on the continent where renaissance masterworks and seminal 20th-century pieces were waiting to captivate us. More so, we also knew that Spain is a country that stands as the main tourist destination in Europe. First, we went to 'The Prado' which is one of the best and most popular art museums in the world. There is an overwhelming collection of masterpieces by renaissance and baroque masters of Spain that is represented by Velazquez and El Greco. Next, we went to Madrid's green heart that is full of elegant gardens, the 'Retiro' which is just a few steps east of the Prado.

Our next visit was the 'Royal Palace'. Built in the mid-1700s for King Philip-V, the Royal Palace is on the site of Madrid's Moorish Alcazar fortress-palace. It is the largest royal palace in western Europe and has a blend of baroque and neoclassical styles. There are works by Goya, Caravaggio, and Velazquez, as well as stunning displays of watches, tapestries, porcelain, and silverware. We saw the string quartet of stradivarius instruments of the world, and the Royal Armoury that included the personal weapons used by Charles-V in the 16th Century. It was a huge palace and probably, it would have taken one full day to see it properly. We enjoyed visiting the Palace, but could not see every aspect of it thoroughly, due to paucity of time.

By the time our visit to the Royal palace was over, we were very hungry and went for lunch to an Asian Garden Restaurant, decorated with bamboo trees and creepers. We thoroughly enjoyed our food and drinks and took several photographs there. Then we proceeded to the 'Grand Square'. This grand square next to the Casa de Correos (Post Office Building) is a popular meeting place. Nearly every Spanish person will recognise the clock at the top of the Casa de Correos. There's an interesting ritual involved too: with every chime, you're supposed to eat a grape for good luck (12 in total). The Spanish people do it when the clock strikes 12 every new year.

We then walked through the 'Gran Via' which is a superb place to loiter around. It's Madrid's entertainment, shopping, and cultural nerve centre, a buzzing avenue often full of life until dawn. But we did not spend much time there, as our evening programme was scheduled for 'Flamenco' show with dinner. We were also not interested to see bull fight, though it is famous in Madrid and preferred to see the stadium only, as the fight took place only in the week ends. Hence, we came back to the hotel and changed our dresses, and went for the Flamenco show, which was scheduled for 8 pm.

Flamenco originated in the southern regions of Spain like in Andalusia, Murcia, and Extremadura, but it's thought to be influenced by many world cultures, including Latin American, Cuban, and Jewish traditions. Though Madrid, the capital city has some of the most famous tables in the country, it did not originate from there. This Spanish art form made up of three parts: guitar playing ("guitarra"), song ("cante"), and dance ("baile"). There are special halls that cropped up in the 1960s, and here we saw a show over a candlelight meal with sangria. Our cab came on time and we reached the show hall in 15minutes. We were escorted and were given a 6-seater table. The ambience was just great and we were served with 2 bottles of wine on our table and each one with a glass of sangria.

Flamenco dance are having many different purposes. This dance is intended to be entertaining, romantic, but at the same time, flamenco is a very emotional style of dance. Flamenco dancers try to express their deepest emotions by using body movements and facial expressions. As the dancers perform, they also clap their hands or kick their feet. Many dancers also snap small percussion handheld instruments called "Castanets". The rhythmic dance and musical show were very enjoyable with varieties of food. Particularly, the dress of the dance is unique, which attracted us a lot. They are made of fabric with different patterns, like polka-dots. Usually, the colours are in combination either black, red or white. They often have ruffles along the skirt and the sleeve. Therefore, their style has to allow lots of body movement. For dancers, the skirts are so designed that they are less tight around the dancer's legs. We could learn a lot about the dance after watching it. It was 2 hours' nonstop show and we thoroughly enjoyed the evening. I was so much fascinated with the hand-held wooden instrument "Castanets" that I bought a pair in the market, the next day and I still play it for my entertainment.

The next day was scheduled for travelling to Valencia by train. We had our breakfast and the cab was ready to drop us at the railway station. The cab was again a black Mercedes SUV. Both my friends Subrat and Deepak were very much impressed to see a black Mercedes SUV on our tour as our ride every single time. Our train was at 9:15 am and we boarded the train in first class, as we had pre-booked our ticket through our travel agent M/s Cox and Kings right from Rourkela. It was again a superfast train and it commuted a distance of 300km in 2hours 15 minutes. The moment the train started moving, Subrat wanted to see whether the pantry car is having the provision of alcoholic beverages or not. When he discovered that it was available, he called Deepak and me for beer. As we had enjoyed the beer in the running train from Lisbon to Porto, the same way we enjoyed it here also. We reached Valencia at around 11:30 am. The journey was very nice and our taxi was ready outside the station to receive us. Again, it was a Mercedes and we went to our hotel and reached noon.

We found that our hotel was a centrally located nice place. We were given a room on the 4th floor. We checked in and then decided to have our lunch. We enquired at our reception about a good restaurant and how to go to the harbour and sea beach site. There were several restaurants with varieties of food, right in front of the hotel, as it was a tourist sea resort. We went to a Thai restaurant and had a fantastic lunch. After lunch, we decided to take a rest in the hotel and again started towards the beach around 4 pm.

We went by bus towards the port area having a beautiful harbour. Just adjacent to the port was the 'Port Sapalaya Beach'. We reached the harbour within 15minutes, which was just 5km from our hotel. It emerged from an old seaport area, which used to be utilized for the export of Tiger nuts, that are grown in that area. In the harbour area, we took a lot of photographs with the backdrop of boats and ships in the sea. Then we walked towards the beautiful sea beach, which had some very nice places to have a drink and also several shops and cafes across the beach. We spent a good amount of time there but were not prepared to bathe in the sea. We went across the beach and finally went to a restaurant to have seafood. We decided to spend some time again on the beach the next day, as it was a nice place. We explored several good eating joints for the next day also and around 9 pm, we came back to our hotel and had wine in the room. Our next day's plan was the city tour.

Valencia has many of the things that attract tourists to Spain, that too all in one place. The city has a vibrant old centre, with many little streets, and splendid medieval buildings like the UNESCO listed 'Lonnja –be-la-Seba.' Like other places, we preferred to take the hop on hop off bus, which we had pre-booked for the city tour. First, we went to 'Lonnja –be-la-Seba' which was a majestic 15th-century building and held as the master piece of Valencian Gothic architecture. This building is the finest monument to Valencia's golden age when the city was one of Europe's main centres for trade and culture. Our next visit was 'Valencia Cathedral' which was built in the 13th century and with neoclassical modifications made over the next few years up to the 14th century. We went inside to see 15th-century Renaissance painting by artists such as the Valencian, Jacomart as well as several from Rome.

Then we proceeded to the 'City of Arts and Science'. The attraction was the staggering ensemble of ultramodern structures that are given an ethereal quality by the reflecting pools that surround them. The whole thing was started in the mid-nineties and the finished in 2005. In these gargantuan buildings, there were several attractions like L'Hemisferic, a planetarium, and I-Max cinema, etc. But for us, the most fascinating place to visit was the 'Oceanografic', which had opened in 2003. It has more than 45,000 individual animals from 500 different species, which was the biggest and best attraction of this large a scale for sea animals in Europe.

The aquarium is organised into 10 zones, each synthesising a distinct environment, using real seawater, pumped from Valencia's waterfront. So, at the arctic tank, we saw 'Beluga whales' swimming in a spacious and thoughtfully designed tank. We also could spot 'Sand tiger sharks' Penguins, Walruses, Dolphins, and Sea lions. Finally, we went to watch the Dolphin show. This 30 minutes Dolphin show was worth watching.

By then, we were tired and after lunch we went to the hotel to relax for an hour. Our main programme and attraction in the evening was to go to 'Sapalaya beach', bathe in the sea and spend some time. That day we went there prepared and had a great time. Rachita and I were comparing the beach with the Miami Beach of the USA. No doubt, Miami Beach was a happening place, but the Sapalaya beach was no less, except for the crowd which was more at Miami. We thoroughly enjoyed ourselves and decided to hop around different restaurants. It was truly an evening well spent. We returned to our hotel around 9 pm and relaxed. Our next day's trip was scheduled for Ibiza by flight at noon. Hence, the next day we leisurely had our breakfast and went to the Valencia airport.

The flight landed at around 1 pm in Ibiza. Since I watch the TV channel on travel, named 'Travel XP' a lot, I knew about the Island Ibiza and was very much impressed. I had told my friends about the place and the nightlife including the beautiful beaches. Hence, we all were very excited about our arrival in Ibiza. Again, riding a beautiful Mercedes SUV, we went to the hotel near St. Antonio Bay named 'Soul house Ibiza Rocks'. The 4-star Soul House Ibiza Hotel boasts an excellent location adjacent to San Antonio Beach.

Many San Antonio sights, including Air Zone Ibiza, were about 15 minutes' walk from the venue. But we did not choose to go to the Air zone, as we preferred to only relax in the bay area. Our hotel was fitted with parquet floors and the rooms featured wireless internet. Throughout the day and night DJ was playing and it was truly a happening place. The infinity pool was on the ground floor and a nice place to swim and chill with a beer. There was a beautiful rooftop bar with a swimming pool too.

After checking in, we went to the poolside and had our lunch, with a view of San Antonio Bay. After lunch, we found that there was an exclusive entry to the beach from the swimming poolside. We spent some time by the side of the pool and then went to the beach. It was a quiet beach and people were simply chilling, bathing, and enjoying there. We were not prepared to bathe that evening and after enjoying for some time, we came back and went to the rooftop. The hotel had 6 floors and on the rooftop bar, we sat and enjoyed the evening. The main attraction was the sunset at 9:20 pm and we had an amazing sight of the sunset. Further, the view of the beach was just great with many boats and cruises dangling in the water. At the same time, the DJ music was further making that place very lively. We started dancing and after enjoying in the rooftop we went to our room at around 10 pm. By then we felt like having some food and we walked through the streets to find a good eating joint. Within 5 minutes we found several good restaurants with varieties of food available. We went to a lively place and spent quality time with good continental food and drink. Our prime aim to go to Ibiza was only to chill and enjoy, without travelling to different sites. The next day, after a beautiful breakfast, we went to the beach and spent several hours bathing. The water was very shallow and quiet. It was the right kind of beach to remain in the water for the whole day and enjoy.

Then we came to the poolside and again started swimming. Beer and food were pettily available and people around us were simply wandering and enjoying near the swimming pool too. Right from morning 11 am till 6 pm we spent the whole day on the beach and the pool. It was a day well spent. We then went to the room and took a rest and again got ready to go to the rooftop and enjoy the sunset. After seeing the sun set and spending some time there, we went to the market side to have dinner and came back at 1 am. It was such a happening place, everyone around there was eating and dancing even at midnight. That was the last day and we did not miss the opportunity to enjoy, though the next day our flight was scheduled at 7:30 am to Barcelona.

After having spent more than 2 unforgettable days in Ibiza, we went to the airport early in the morning and flew to Barcelona. We landed in Barcelona at around 8:30 am and found that the airport is huge as compared to Valencia and Ibiza. We went to the hotel by as usual a Mercedes Benz cab. The climate was very nice and the city seemed to be very vibrant. On our arrival in Barcelona, we were thrilled and found some differences from the capital city Madrid. Catalonia's vibrant capital, Barcelona is a stunning seaside city that flaunts its beauty and sunny lifestyle. Gorgeous scenery, breath-taking architecture, and superb cultural attractions made it more alluring. Of course, the Mediterranean climate added to the charm. The famous architect Antoni Gaudí left an everlasting mark on Barcelona with his avant-garde surrealist buildings. Several such buildings were UNESCO heritage sites. Capital of Catalonia and Spain's second city, Barcelona is utterly incomparable to any other city. On the first day of our arrival and after checking in the hotel, we first visited the sandy beaches near the harbour, and lingered over leisurely meals on outdoor terraces. The harbour area was very huge and it was fantastic to spend time there with the sea breeze. It was also nice to find hidden town squares, where street musicians strummed melodies on famous Spanish guitars and delightful surprises, which awaited us at every turn.

That evening, we went to 'Basilica de la Sagrada Familia', one of Europe's most unconventional churches, which was a spectacular basilica and very famous site in Barcelona. The UNESCO-listed Basilica de la Sagrada Familia stands in the northern part of the city, dominating its surroundings with its 18 spindly towers soaring high above all other monuments. The Basilica of the Sacred Family is also known in Spanish by its official name: Temple Expiatori de la Sagrada Família. After visiting the place, it was around 8 pm and we preferred to come back to the hotel, as we had gotten up very early that day to board our flight from Ibiza.

The next day, we had the ticket in the hop on hop off bus and after breakfast, we started for the tour. Barcelona had so many places to visit that, we decided to be selective and go to the places of our choice. That day, we first went to Barri Gotic (Gothic Quarter). That place was having several trendy bars in the narrow medieval streets. It was a nice place to visit and as it was morning time, we did not want to go to any bar. While travelling in the bus further, we found that the huge bullfight stadium was closed and from a distance, it was explained by the guide that, the bullfight was stopped in Barcelona in the year 2010, though the bullfight is famous in Spain. It was very surprising for us, that there was a distinctive difference in culture between Madrid and Barcelona, including the look of the people.

After having a good ride on the bus, we got down near a park, where we went to the cable car. The Montjuïc Cable Car (officially Telefèric de Montjuïc, in Catalan) which is a gondola lift in Barcelona. The cable car runs from a lower terminus adjacent to the Montjuïc Park upper station of the Montjuïc funicular and climbs higher up the Montjuïc hill to a terminal near the Montjuïc Castle on the summit of the hill. At its midpoint, the line executes a 90-degree turn and the cabins pass through Mirador station. The cable car was originally put into service in 1970, replacing a former upper stage of the Montjuïc funicular. The cable car line is 752 metres in length and climbs a vertical distance of 84.55 metres at a speed of 2.5 m/s. The ride was very thrilling and I recapitulated and compared it with Quebec rope way ride, in Canada. This Barcelona ride was better than the ride in Quebec, Canada. From the top of the castle, we could see the old cannons and the sea harbour site from the top, which was a spectacular sight. After visiting such a great site, we next went to the world-famous Football club 'Barcelona FC'. Though, we could not go inside, but saw it from outside and it filled our hearts with delight.

Then, we proceeded to 'La Rambla' which was Barcelona's Social Hub. The heart of Barcelona's social life is found in La Rambla, a broad, tree-shaded avenue that divides the Old Town into two parts. La Rambla stretches from the Plaça de Catalunya, where the beautiful Romanesque 12th-century Convent of Santa Anna stands. This wide street, featuring expansive pedestrian sidewalks, is lined with shops, restaurants, and outdoor cafes, making it one of the most popular hangouts in the city. During the day, many locals are found here doing their everyday shopping at the Mercat de la Boqueria, and at night, groups of friends and families take their evening stroll on La Rambla to enjoy the fresh air and lively ambience. On the day, we as visitors enjoyed those areas to a great extent. We also enjoyed to live music, a mime show and many other impromptu street performances in Barcelona, which fascinated us a lot.

To visit all the good tourist places in Barcelona was virtually impossible and around 7 pm, we were extremely tired and were also hungry. We found an Indian restaurant named 'Gandhi' and went there to have Mughlai food with kebab. We had a great time with a fulfilled dinner. Talking to the owner of the restaurant in Hindi language, after a long time was just great. The next day was the last day in Barcelona and also in Spain. We had the programme to go to the 'Montserrat'.

The next day since our visit was in the afternoon, we leisurely got up and just relaxed after breakfast. For the programme of the 'Iconic Montserrat in Catalonia', our cab arrived at 2 pm and we travelled for about an hour from our hotel to reach the spot. Montserrat is located approximately 48 km away from Barcelona which makes it perfect for a day out. Since we went by cab and hence parked the cab at the free Monistrol Vila parking lot. We had our ticket booked earlier through M/s Cox and Kings for the half-day tour of Montserrat, which included the Rack rail ticket, the entrance ticket, and many more. Finally, we took the Rack Railway (Cremallera de Montserrat). The experience of Rack rail was amazing, as it was moving almost vertical and we were thrilled to have such a ride.

 At 1236 meters height, this spiritual retreat is the highest point in and around Barcelona. It is surrounded by a natural park and shaped by nature's elements, the Montserrat rock formations which was a breath-taking panoramic view across Catalonia. It was truly a spectacular place. Apart from the picturesque surroundings and gorgeous Santa Maria de Montserrat, in the abbey itself there are also two trails to take around the mountains with panoramic views of the valley. Also referred to as Black Madonna, this Romanesque, wood-carved statue has a monumental significance in Montserrat. We also went to the 'Montserrat Museum' which houses six permanent collections of more than 1,300 artefacts as well as temporary displays. All those were just amazing experiences at the top of the hill.

There was a huge souvenir shop with snacks and alcoholic beverages available there. We bought some souvenirs and to our surprise, we had free coupons for some alcohol which was included in our tour. Since the ladies did not take it, Subrat, Deepak and I had the opportunity to have it and enjoyed it thoroughly, at that eternal site.

The site was so attractive that we took hundreds of photographs and overall, we enjoyed the place. We came back to the hotel at around 9 pm. The next day was our return journey to Mumbai, India. After such a wonderful trip, we were not feeling like coming back home.

The next day we started from our hotel quite leisurely as our flight from Barcelona to Paris was scheduled at around 1 pm. We reached Paris around 3 pm and our next flight to Mumbai was at 8 pm Paris time. We had deliberately chosen such layover in Paris. We did all our shopping from the duty-free shops and had the evening coffee at the airport. It was a great time spent in the airport and we finally boarded the flight for our return journey to Mumbai, India.

The flight duration was around 9 hours and we reached Mumbai at around 8:30 am (IST). We had a great time on the flight discussing the trip to Portugal and Spain. My nephew Anshuman had come to the airport in Mumbai and we stayed in their house for a day to relax. Subrat and Deepak also went to their relatives' place and the next day we came to Bhubaneswar. From there, we came back to Rourkela, and then I realised that I had retired and had to do many unfinished jobs, that included my post-retirement activities.

Chapter 14:

Desert in UAE, Rainforest & Cruise in Malaysia, and George Michael on My Mind

As, I superannuated in May'18 and immediately travelled Spain and Portugal, some important activities, such as looking for a house to live in at Rourkela, was in abeyance. I was supposed to leave the quarter provided by my company, within 2 months' post retirement, as per the rule in vogue. It was all to gather, a different experience to explore for a house, after having spent more than 60 years in different houses provided by our company in the steel city of Rourkela. Finally, we got a decent flat at Jagda, in a centrally located place, near NIT. We settled down after discarding several articles of our old house, which we had accumulated for ages. We also bought many new articles, compatible with the new flat at Jagda. Though it was a different experience, at the same time it was a very nice and exciting to settle in a flat and start a new life. Rachita found it, somewhat difficult to adjust initially, as her school was a bit far from our new residence, which created a further problem for her. But very soon, mode of transport to school was resolved and gradually we got acclimatized to the place and started enjoying the process of getting settled there. My brothers and my mother also came and stayed with us several times and appreciated the location and the house.

The next important aspect was to make own self busy after superannuation. I had personally decided not to join any steel industry or for that matter any industry after my superannuation, though I had got several good offers. I stuck to my decision and eventually wanted to do something for my alma mater. I got elected and became the President of my alumni association named 'National Institute of Technology Alumni Association' (NITRAA). Also, I started another passion which is writing and taking sessions on both technical and non-technical areas. Fortunately, I got the opportunity to become a guest faculty in the Indian Institute of Production Management (IIPM), Kansbahal, as I was already a guest faculty to the Management Training Institute, SAIL at Ranchi. It gave me immense pleasure to take classes and also got the opportunity to visit several places in India. Because of my sessions, I got to visit new places like Assam, Meghalaya, Surat, etc., which I had never visited earlier, though I have visited many other places in India.

But at the same time, my other passion of travelling to different places abroad had not dampened, and I thought of continuing my prime passion. Of course, initially, five of my friends and I visited different places in the coastal district of Odisha by SUV (XUV 500) in the first week of October and thoroughly enjoyed it. Thereafter, during the Puja holidays of 2018, Rachita and I travelled to Rajasthan, which was a new visiting state for us. We visited Mount Abu, Udaipur, and Jaipur for about ten days. It was a fantastic trip.

In the meantime, my urge to travel foreign land got triggered, and we decided to travel to Sri Lanka. We made all plans to go to Sri Lanka in May 2019, during Rachita's school holidays. My co-brother-in-law, Manoj, from the USA was posted at Abu Dhabi in UAE for a year on some assignment. So, before going to Sri Lanka, I decided to go and visit him. Rachita was not free from school during that period, which was the month of February and incidentally, the tourist season for UAE. Hence, I decided to go alone to UAE. Manoj was staying alone in a suite in Novotel Hotel in Abu Dhabi. I booked a hotel in Dubai to get the UAE visa easily and went to Abu Dhabi via Cochin. It was a Wednesday that I travelled to Abu Dhabi, as suggested by Manoj. I travelled via Cochin by Indigo airlines. Though it was not a very luxurious flight, but was convenient for me. I had to pay for the food and beverages on the flight. It was a 4 hours 30 minutes' travel distance and I reached Abu Dhabi at around 5 pm. The airport was very beautiful and the most exciting part was that Manoj gave me a surprise and came to receive me to the airport. I went to his hotel in his car.

The roads were extremely good and very clean. Manoj suddenly took his car near a petrol pump, even though there was enough petrol in his car. There was a car cleaning/washing place which was adjacent to the petrol pump. Though the car was not very dirty, he got it washed. I asked him, what was so urgent that he came to a car washing place. Manoj explained that there is a fine imposed for 500 Dirham, if the car is dirty, but only 35 Dirham is charged for washing and cleaning the car. Though I had travelled to several countries and places, I had never seen such a rule in any place or country. After car washing, we reached the hotel and went to his room. It was a fantastic suite. By that time, I was famished. He offered me a can of beer and fruits. I felt relaxed, as I had started at 7 am (India time) from Bhubaneswar. That evening we simply chilled and watched TV.

The next day Manoj went to his office and asked me to be ready by 2:30 pm and he came from his office around 2 pm. At 2:45 pm a SUV came and we went for the desert safari. It was a unique experience to go for the safari. Several high-powered SUVs assembled in the middle of the desert. The landscape created of its own in the sand was unique and we took a lot of photographs. After that, the actual safari started. The stunt done by the expert driver in the desert was very thrilling. About 30 minutes later, we reached a camel breeding place and could see hundreds of camels owned by some sheikh. Manoj and I were loitering in the desert nearby and observed something interesting. A sheikh with his family came with a SUV and got down there. He took out some remote-control transmitters and gave some signal. An Arabic falcon came flying and sat near the sheikh. A receiver was fitted in its leg and the falcon came to its master in the deep desert. The sheikh had brought several dove birds in a cage and took 2 out of them and cut their head. He fed only the head portion to the falcon. It was such a new experience for us, that we started talking to him to find out what exactly he did. The sheikh explained that the falcon loves to eat the head portion of the dove and becomes very loyal to the master. When asked about the remaining portion of the dove, he further explained that they would cook those and eat with their family. We took a lot of photographs with them and the falcon too. It was truly an interesting and new experience for us.

We then again proceeded with our SUV in the desert and navigated several twists and turns on the sand. Finally, we were taken to a beautiful desert camp. It was around 6:30 pm that we reached there and we found it very interesting. Complimentary soft drinks and alcoholic beverages were available in the deep desert. We were given some complimentary drinks and subsequently had to buy as per our choice. There were several stalls for entertainment and at the centre, there was a big stage for dance and music. Buffet dinner was provided and we sat around the stage to watch the entertainment programme. With beautiful light and music, the programme started with belly dance and acrobatics with fire juggling, etc. It was an amazing experience inside the deep desert and it continued up to 9:30 pm. Then we returned to our hotel.

The next day was a Friday and Manoj had Friday and Saturday as holidays. I had booked a hotel in Dubai and the next morning, we started for Dubai. The road from Abu Dhabi to Dubai was just fantastic and cars were moving at 120 to 130 km/hr. As per the rule, one could drive at 140 km/hour. Even though Manoj had more than 2 decades of driving experience in USA, he was also bit surprised during his initial stay in Abu Dhabi, to drive so fast. We commuted the distance of about 130 km in one and half hours as we were travelling very leisurely. I being a traveller, had seen all major land marks of Dubai on the TV channel 'Travelxp' and also knew about hotel 'Atlantics'. Having seen several times about hotel Atlantics in the TV, I was having a great desire to go there. Manoj also had not seen that area and immediately agreed. We directly went near hotel Atlantis and were astonished to see the gigantic hotel by the side of the sea.

The road leading to the hotel was very wide and the pavement was very clean, with lot of greenery, from where the beautiful sight of the sea could be enjoyed. After spending some time near the sea, we went inside the Hotel Atlantis. The beautiful garden and the overall ambience were just great. There was a big shopping complex with nice restaurants, having varieties of food available there. Manoj and I chose to go to a restaurant with oriental food with alcoholic beverages. Getting alcohol in Dubai was a difficult task, but we got it in that restaurant, of course after paying very heavily. It was very enjoyable, and after lunch, we returned to our hotel and checked in around 4 pm. It was a nice hotel named 'Grand Central'. We parked our car and relaxed in the hotel. From 6 pm, Manoj had a conference call up to

7:30 pm, I had a peg 'Jack Daniel' whisky along with some appetisers, ordered from the hotel, and then around 9 pm we went around walking through the streets for dinner. The streets were full of lights and well decorated with huge billboards. I somewhat had a feeling of New York. The climate was very pleasant in February and it was a different experience in a country like UAE. We went to a garden restaurant and had several varieties of seafood. We could not visualize the quantity served and finally could not finish our food. After spending about an hour for dinner, we went around walking through the streets, and around midnight, we came back to the hotel.

The next morning, our programme was to go towards the most iconic building Burj Khalifa. Accordingly, after having breakfast, we went to that area. First Manoj suggested going to the Dubai Mall. It was so huge that it was impossible to go round the entire mall. Probably it is the biggest mall in the world. We then went to the fountain area, which is the central place in between 'Burj Khalifa' and 'Dubai Mall'. It was an amazing place to spend time in, watching the dancing fountain, and many other activities. The view of 'Burj Khalifa' was great from there and we took several photographs. It was truly a happening place and worth visiting. We thought of going to the top of 'Burj Khalifa', but seeing the very long queue, we got disappointed and dropped the idea. After going to the top of Berlin tower, CN Tower, and Eiffel tower, Burj Khalifa was nothing new for me, except for the height.

We started our return journey towards Abu Dhabi from Dubai around 2 pm and directly went to a harbour area near Abu Dhabi. Manoj took me to 'Al Mina' Fish market, which was the largest fish market in Abu Dhabi. Hundreds of varieties of seafood were available. The best part of the market was to choose the raw fish, crab, prawn, or anything available, and get it cooked, grilled then and there. We not only ate in that place but also got the seafood cooked & packed. Back in the hotel, we took a few glasses of beer, had that seafood, and slept. The overall experience was just great. The next day Manoj went to his office in the morning and explained to me about all the facilities available in the hotel including the swimming pool and health club. He also provided me with his iPad. I googled about the Gulf and particularly about the UAE. It was very fascinating to read and know all those things about the countries.

At around 11 am, I went for a sauna bath and swam in the pool with a glass of beer. That was a nice experience. The next day also Manoj went to his office and I went to the backyard garden of the hotel with beautiful palm and date trees. I sat with a book and started reading in total isolation in a serene atmosphere with nobody around. I rediscovered that I can live and spend time in solitude, that too qualitatively. While sitting on the wooden bench, I saw a dove flying from a palm tree. I started watching the bird very minutely. It went and again came back after 4 to 5 minutes to its nest. Then two doves, both male, and female went and again flew and came after about 10 minutes. I could discover that they got some food for their babies in the nest. I observed the activity for more than 1 hours and was totally engrossed. I did not even realise that it was past 2 pm and was my lunchtime. It was extremely enjoyable to observe the doves on that day, which probably I would never have observed if I would not have been alone.

Manoj came a bit early on that day from his office and we were relaxing in the drawing-room, watching TV. I suddenly found that it started raining. Though the intensity of rain was not very heavy, it continued for more than 2 hours. Manoj was surprised to see the rain and said I have been very lucky for him, to see the rain, which is extremely rare in Abu Dhabi. Those were the lifetime experiences that I cannot forget for life.

The next day was my scheduled return flight from Abu Dhabi to New Delhi. So, we thought of going to the Grand Mosque after the rain. Around 8 pm we went there and by then the climate was clear and cold. I could not comprehend that a mosque could be so huge and beautiful. The entry to the main building was through horizontal and inclined escalators. The pass for the entrance was done through a computer and was in high-tech mode. It was amazing to see such arrangements in a mosque, which was better than any airport, worldwide. We saw every nook and corner, including the main prayer hall. The carpet laid in the prayer hall was wall-to-wall carpeting and was probably the largest in UAE. The place was extremely beautiful with lighting at night. We then came to the hotel and had some food and drinks and watched the TV.

 The next day my flight was scheduled in the evening. Manoj dropped me at the airport, which took around 20 minutes from the hotel. After check-in, there was sufficient time and thought of going to the lounge. It was such a beautiful lounge with varieties of alcoholic beverages and food. I spent more than an hour of quality time and then went to my departure gate. My return flight destination was booked for Delhi by Air India. The flight was not only full but also overcrowded. There was a lot of noise inside the aircraft. I had a very horrible experience and finally reached New Delhi around 5 am IST. I went to my daughter Anooja's place at Gurugram. I stayed there for 3 days and came back to Rourkela via Bhubaneswar. In a nutshell, the visit to Abu Dhabi and Dubai was a great experience.

A couple of days later, I started planning for Sri Lanka, as per my original plan, through M/s Cox and Kings. I wanted to visit the southwest part of Sri Lanka including Colombo. I was very much attracted to go there as both my daughters had visited Sri Lanka and had recommended it strongly. The place like "Ministry of Crab", as a great eating joint, the beautiful mangroves in Bentota were the attractions that I had planned to visit. I had also added "Virgin tea plantation", which in other words is also called "White tea plantation", in my tour. This variety is a rare variety of tea grown in Sri Lanka, by the side of the sea. I had already booked the air ticket and had given advance to the travel agent. Our scheduled departure was on 30th May'2019. But to our bad luck, a series of unfortunate bomb blasts happened in Sri Lanka on the 24th of April, and we had to cancel the trip. Though the travel agent M/s Cox and Kings returned the advance amount, I lost a lot of money on my flight ticket. But I consider the episode as a typical experience that is engraved in my mind and still have kept my plan to go to Sri Lanka.

Subsequently, in one of our friend's get to gather, some of our close friends decided to go to Thailand and Malaysia. Since I had visited Thailand in 1998, I wanted to go only to Malaysia and my friends agreed. We thought of travelling in October '2019. Again, I approached M/s Cox and Kings for our tour through the Flexi holidays scheme. After several rounds of discussion, except my friend Prakash, all others dropped out. We made plans for Genting Highland, Kuala Lumpur, and Langkawi Island. We chose the direct flight for Kuala Lumpur from Bhubaneswar by Air Asia. Going from Bhubaneswar for an international flight was a fantastic experience and a dream come true. Prakash and I boarded the flight at around midnight and reached Kuala Lumpur at around 6:30 am Malaysia time. The duration of the flight was around 4 ½ hours. Though the flight was not that good, it was fun going to the place from our own home state.

On arrival, the immigration was done quite fast and the cab was waiting outside the airport for us. We straight went to Genting Highland via Batu caves. Though we were very tired, we did not feel the pinch, as we were very thrilled and in a very good state of mind. We got down at Batu Caves, which took about an hour from the airport. It was a sunny day and the climate was very pleasant. It was here that we saw the Kartikeswar statue. The height of the statue was 140 feet. It is the tallest statue in Malaysia and is located at the Sri Murugan Perumal Kovil at the foot of Batu Caves. It was a beautiful sight, with several other temples. We had our South Indian breakfast at that place and then proceeded towards Genting Highlands. It took us around an hour to reach our hotel. It was a wonder to see the hotel. It was nothing but the largest hotel in the world named 'First World Hotel'. The hotel lobby is so huge that it seems like an airport check-in counter. The hotel has 7351 rooms and has found its place in the Guinness Book of World Records.

We went to our room and took a rest for some time, before we went for breakfast. After breakfast, we thoroughly explored the hotel. It was not only a hotel but a tourist spot by itself, for those who are staying in other places of Genting Highland. There was a big market complex along with an amusement park. It also had a big casino and a big lobby with fantastic lighting. It took about 2 hours for thorough exploration. Then we had lunch and took a rest, as the previous night, we had travelled on the plane, we were tired. We had a pre-booked ropeway ride from our hotel. In the evening, after standing in a long queue, we boarded the ropeway ride named "Genting Skyway". It was around 3.4

km long and the journey was exhilarating, having a breath-taking view of numerous landmarks within the highlands, including a 120-million-year-old tropical rain forest. The one-way ride was about 30 minutes and during the ride, we were virtually passing through the clouds. We landed at the base and roamed around in the nearby place and had ice cream. Again, we boarded the same cable car, as we had the return ticket from the same starting point, which was the hotel in which we were staying. During our return journey, it was dark and we enjoyed the lighting of the whole area and the landscape. Before we went to our room, we wanted to see the casino and I did not find it very interesting like Kathmandu. Hence after dinner at McDonalds, we went to our room and stayed in the hotel.

The next morning, after breakfast, we started for Kuala Lumpur, by the same vehicle and the same driver, who had dropped us on the day of our arrival, whose name was Ganesh. We reached by 1 pm at our hotel, which was centrally located in the city. After lunch, we travelled the nearby places by walking through the streets. The next day, we had a sightseeing tour. We went to different temples, mosques, markets, and other tourist palaces. But, our first visit was to a chocolate manufacturing company named Harriston. They explained how chocolate is made out of the cocoa extract. Finally, we bought some varieties of chocolate after the tasting. We then visited the King's palace named 'Istana Negara' which was very beautiful, with horse riding guards, standing in front of the palace gate. We took a lot of photographs as the climate was sunny and breezy. After the visit, in the afternoon we went to a pub in the Bukit Bintang area, famous for its pubs and nightlife. Since the next day, we had a plan to go to Langkawi Island we preferred to go to the pub during day time instead of a night visit. It was a cosy pub with nice draught beer, that we had with grilled fish.

Our next trip was to the world-famous Petronas Twin Tower. It was a cloudy afternoon and we had the pre-booked ticket with us. It was enthralling to see the tall twin tower of 452 meters. We went to the top floor at a height of 375 meters. The whole of Kuala Lumpur was visible from the deck. Furthermore, the day having cloudy weather, the cloud was moving in our height. It was an awesome experience. In front of the tower, the beautiful garden with cascade was having several varieties of flowers. The whole area was not only beautiful but also a happening place. From there, we went to a local market that had a typical Malaysian feeling. We bought several types of fruits including Mangosteen, which is a typical tropical fruit. I had eaten Mangosteen, first time at Mettupalayam, when we had visited Ooty (Udhagamandalam) in 1986 and subsequently I had developed a taste for it. I ate that fruit even in several wedding parties and I made it a point to organise it during the wedding ceremony of my daughter Anooja. However, after spending a great day, we came back to our hotel, with those fruits and I must say that, it was overall a wonderful day spent in Kuala Lumpur.

The next day, we had the flight to Langkawi Island. We had booked the 12:30 pm flight so that we can start leisurely from the hotel. It took us only an hour to reach Langkawi from Kuala Lumpur. The cab was waiting outside the airport, we came out of the small but beautiful airport and boarded the cab. Our hotel booking was at 'Aloft Langkawi Pantai'. We reached the hotel within 45 minutes and were amazed to see it. We had a sea-facing room in the hotel with a beautiful balcony. Our room door entry side was the corridor and in front of the corridor was the rain forest, which was extremely beautiful. The very first glimpse of the hotel was truly great. We settled down and then walked through the lanes near the hotel. It was a serene and calm place. The climate was also nice. We went to a garden restaurant and had our lunch. We then took a rest in our room. In the evening, in the ground floor lobby, a live band was in attendance. There was a beautiful bar too. I and my friend Prakash sat in the bar of the lobby and had a couple of draught beers with grilled chicken. I also requested the band to sing some of my favourite songs by George Michael. It was a lovely evening on the very first day. On a subsequent morning, Prakash and I went to the nearby sea beach after breakfast at around 11 am. The hotel provided us with bathing towels. The sea was very shallow with clear water and white sand. But there was a board having a display, "Beware of Jellyfish". Initially, I was scared, but to our surprise, lifeguards were giving free service and guided us as to which part of the water was safe. Prakash didn't opt to bathe, but I was prepared with my swimming costume and enjoyed bathing in the sea. There was a big banyan tree by the side of the beach, where we chilled. The backdrop of the sea was full of beautiful, lush green mountains and the whole atmosphere was very enjoyable. We returned at around 1:30 pm and took a rest at the hotel after lunch.

We had the 'Cruise with dinner' trip on the same day from 5 pm to 10 pm. We were ready by 4:15 pm and the car came to our hotel at around 4:30 pm. It was only 20 minutes' distance to the harbour, which was the starting point of our cruise. We boarded the small cruise at around 5 pm. All our co-passengers were from different parts of the world. In total around 30 people were there on the cruise. The cruise started towards the deep sea along with the passengers and the crew members. Since our trip was inclusive of dinner, the moment our cruise started, one guy started the barbeque preparation. Unlimited alcohol including beer was served on the board. Both the onward and return journey was around 2 hours, full of merry and mirth. The view of the setting sun with a backdrop of the small hill-like islands was just amazing. To add to our enjoyment, at the same time, the lifeguards on the board fixed a big net at the backside of the cruise. That facilitated anyone to dip half the body in the sea and enjoy, just by sitting and holding the net, while the cruise was moving. I was prepared for such adventurous bathing and did that with the help of the lifeguards. I cruised through the sea water on the net. It was a thrilling experience with that matching speed of the cruise, which was full of excitement.

After that stunt, we were invited for dinner. The dinner was served with several varieties of cuisines including the barbeque items with chicken, shrimps, etc., along with fried squid. By then, we were feeling hungry and had a fantastic dinner along with the last round of cocktails. By the time we returned to the seashore, it was around 9 pm. We reached the hotel around 10 pm. I, as usual, could not resist the live band music in our hotel and spent about an hour there, before going to the room.

The next day, we had the half a day tour of Langkawi. Our first trip was to Langkawi Wildlife Park. It took us about an hour to reach the park and the road leading to the park was full of the rainforest. The Park was a tropical garden with over 2500 exotic birds from 150 species. We took a lot of photographs of the animals and birds. The best attraction was that, we were given a handful of grains and hundreds of small birds ate that from our palm. That was a typical and fantastic experience. Then we came to one of Lagakawi's biggest landmarks, Dataran Lang, also known as the Eagle Square. This square has been built, in about 19 acres' area. Small ponds, fountains and a big eagle are some of the main attractions in that area. The Eagle Square is a square on Langkawi near the port where ferries sail in and out. The giant statue of an eagle at the centre is poised to take flight. The eagle is about 40 feet tall. The reddish-brown eagle was built as a symbol of the island. According to folklore, Langkawi's name was derived from two Malay words- helang which means eagle, and kawi which means reddish brown. It is one of Langkawi's most recognizable iconic sights. We spent about an hour and we found it to be a lovely place to visit.

From that place, we went to a duty-free shop. Langkawi is a duty-free island. The duty-free shop was very huge and I had not seen such a huge shop in any international airport in the world. It was probably, the cheapest duty-free shop I had ever visited and that too on the island itself. We bought only chocolates and alcohol from there. But one can buy only one litre of alcohol and I preferred to buy a single malt whiskey named 'Dalmore'. From there, we started for our hotel. Prakash and I took a rest and I went for a body massage to a nearby spa. After a good massage, I went to the rooftop swimming pool. It was around 5 pm and I spent more than an hour in the pool and had a couple of drinks in the pool side bar. It was extremely enjoyable and refreshing to swim after a full body massage and on top of it, having a couple of drinks. That evening, we had a plan to go to a seafood joint and as I am extremely fond of seafood, I ordered crab. Like any good seafood joint, they would show the crab or fish as per your choice and cook accordingly. A similar arrangement was available and I chose a crab of around 600 grams and asked to cook only the meat. He prepared an awesome dish of the crab. As, Prakash is not fond of sea food, we also asked to prepare chicken dish. Prakash is not at all a seafood lover and he was looking at my eating style with awe. For me, the food was out of the world. Though he ate some vegetarian stuff and chicken, both of us relished the food. We came to the hotel and as usual, sat in the lobby and enjoyed live music. That night being the last, we sat in the bar up to late and enjoyed the evening thoroughly.

The next day was our return flight to Kuala Lumpur and from Kuala Lumpur to Bhubaneswar. We had taken the flight from Langkawi to

Kuala Lumpur at 1:30 pm as our flight from Kuala Lumpur to Bhubaneswar was scheduled at 10 pm. By 3 pm we were at Kuala Lumpur airport and we had sufficient time to spend at the airport. I had my priority pass for lounge entry and before the security, I went to the lounge to spent some time with good food drinks. At 7 pm we passed through the security check and did some last-minute shopping from the duty-free shop. After shopping also, we had sufficient time and we preferred to spend some time in a bar and thoroughly enjoyed. We boarded the same Air Asia flight and reached Bhubaneswar at 12:30 am. The overall Malaysia trip was just amazing.

Chapter 15:

The Vision of a Middle-Class Man

My next plan was to go to Turkey in April or May of 2020, which would have been a trip with family. However, from January 2020, we were listening about Corona Virus in Wuhan, China. I had been to Bhubaneswar on 14th of March 2020 to attend the marriage reception of one of my friends Nabin's son. The reception party was on 15th March and on the same morning it was announced by the Government, to limit the number of guests in any gathering or party. However, we went in the evening for the party and thoroughly enjoyed with limited number of friends and guests. On 17th morning I returned to Rourkela by road, along with another friend Pradeep. On 23rd of March, national lockdown was declared for the Covid pandemic.

It was unlike anything we had ever experienced. We would be glued to the TV most of the time for updates and news. The pandemic subsequently spread in our country and finally not only our country, but also, the whole world came to a standstill. We all remained confined in the four walls of our houses. It was absolutely a new situation and my travel within India as a tourist and for taking sessions & classes, which I had been doing after my retirement, came to a halt. Amidst all the chaos and uncertainty, my passion for travelling abroad also faced a stand still. However, during some relaxation of lock down across the country, we visited Bangalore to our elder daughter Anisha in October'2020 and Gurugram to younger daughter Anooja in July'2021.But, when total normalcy is restored after the pandemic, apart from Turkey, my first place of visit would be Sri Lanka, which, I had to cancel in 2019 at the final stage. Secondly, I still have the plan to visit USA again, as there are several places in my mind, which I could not visit earlier in my previous two visits, USA being a very vast country.

Having all the bad experience of the pandemic, in the first week of, April 2020, I thought of writing about my experiences, which I had accomplished in my life. Particularly, being a middle-class common man, how I could fulfil my dream of travelling abroad, that too several countries and have an enriched experience. Initially, I thought that, it would be impossible for me to write a book, about my experiences, which would be so voluminous. But I always believed "Where there is a will, there is a way". What further boosted my spirits was the book "The Alchemist" by Paulo Coelho, particularly this line from the book:

"And, when you want something, all the universe conspires in helping you to achieve it."

From 4th of April 2020, I started writing about my experiences which took more than a year to complete. It is probably the pandemic, which pushed and compelled me to remain at home, most of the time and I could rediscover myself, in a different form. I sometimes wonder, that I could patiently write such a book for more than a year and hence, this book is very precious and close to my heart.

Prabodh Ranjan Padhee

SAbout the Book

This book is not only a vivid guide to making the most out of your passion of travelling even when you belong to a humble background, but also a heartfelt memoir of the life of a middle-class man. It is the narration of the experiences of the author as he anchors his responsibilities as the head of the family while also being the person who fulfils his own desire and follows his passion. The book cruises through decades of achievements, big and small; through rivers of smiles and tears alike; as the author travels through the world, taking the readers along with him on this beautiful journey. The book is nothing but the journey of the dream of a child that was most graciously brought to fruition during his adulthood. All the events mentioned in the book are real instances from the author's life presented to the reader with utmost sincerity and frankness.

About the Author

Prabodh Ranjan Padhee is a passionate traveller and writer who hails from the small steel town of Rourkela. He completed graduation in Mechanical Engineering from Regional Engineering College, Rourkela (Presently National Institute of Technology, Rourkela) in the year 1980. He joined the public sector company, Steel Authority of India Limited (SAIL) as a Management Trainee that very year and superannuated in 2018 as the Chief General Manager (Erstwhile General Manager) of Rourkela Steel Plant, SAIL. He went on to co-author a book titled *"Process Modelling for Steel Industry"*, which has become an acclaimed book for steel industry and academic perspective. He has also published various articles in reputed international journals such as Wiley and Springer Nature. He has served as the Guest Faculty of several reputed institutions all over India and is a regular panellist in various seminars and webinars. He has also presented papers in International Conference, which has been published by Springer Nature. This book is his debut *"Non-fiction"* book, where he has attempted to amalgamate his greatest passion, which is **travelling and writing**, in the honest possible manner.